THE EFFECTIVE INTERPRETING SERIES

Simultaneous Interpreting from English

Carol J. Patrie

San Diego, California

The Effective Interpreting Series: Simultaneous Interpreting from English

Producer: Joe W. Dannis

Printed in the United States of America

Published by DawnSignPress

Rosetta Stone image © Copyright The British Museum. The Rosetta Stone appears throughout the series as a symbol of translation's importance to mankind. The basalt slab was discovered in July 1799 in the small Egyptian village of Rosette on the western delta of the Nile. The stone's inscription in hieroglyphic, demotic, and Greek languages led to a crucial breakthrough in research regarding Egyptian hieroglyphs. This key to "translating silent images" into a living language symbolizes the importance of accurate transmissions of messages from one language into another.

The Rosetta Stone now resides in the British Museum in London.

Cover Design: Greg Smith

ISBN: 978-1-58121-162-7

10 9 8 7 6 5 4 3 2

For Cameron Michael Alsop
—the Light of my life.

Acknowledgments

As I look back over the evolution of *The Effective Interpreting Series,* I see that I was inspired, literally "in a flash" to design and create these interpreter education materials. Fortunately for me, and for the field of interpreter education, Joe Dannis believed in me and my vision from the outset. We have been working together on these materials since 1995. I am grateful to Joe and his unwavering commitment to my creativity. He has had the courage and generosity to support this long-term and ongoing project with all its unexpected twists and turns. He is the steady hand in the background behind *The Effective Interpreting Series.*

I experience gratitude again as I realize that many people at DawnSignPress worked diligently and patiently over time to bring this book to publication. I thank the marketing staff, convention staff, editorial staff, customer service staff, and warehouse staff for their kindnesses and support.

I am grateful to all the speakers who took time from their busy schedules to be videotaped for this project. They are Thyra Benoit, Marquessa Brown, David Burnight, Eugene Corbett, Arlene Fong Craig, Jaime Coronado, Jeff Hardison, Bobbi Jordan, Peter Leary, Amber Lewnes, Chris Lewnes Lorraine Oldham, Ella Perkin, Janet Perkin, and Leslie Rach.

One of the hallmarks of DawnSignPress products is high quality video. The video associated with this book is no exception. High quality videos are essential in interpreter education. I thank all those involved in filming the video including Yoon Lee and Andy Hall. The editing of this video makes it unique and I am excited about the fine work accomplished by Joseph Josselyn and Dan Veltri.

I offer a warm and heartfelt thanks to Rebecca Ryan who has seen all five books in *The Effective Interpreting Series* from first draft to publication. This is a huge feat and she has undertaken the development and editing of each volume with insight and precision. She has remained dedicated to the project with devotion and clarity and we have learned to dance some intricate steps together along the way, alternating as leader and follower. She stands cheerfully beside me through the good and bad weather of a writer's life. Once again she has borne witness to the birth of a book.

I am especially grateful for the tremendous amount of positive feedback on previous volumes in *The Effective Interpreting Series* from teachers, students, and interpreters. I am thrilled to bring you the fifth volume in the series. I hope you will enjoy it and I look forward to your valuable feedback.

Contents

Preface

When I became a professional interpreter in 1968, interpreter education was rare. Since that time, interpreter education has made great strides. Soon after my first year of professional interpreting in 1968, I began attempting to teach interpreting. From that time to now, I have been building a store of ideas and materials related to teaching interpretation. I am pleased to share with you my 35 years of experience. I am one of the developers of the Master of Arts in Interpretation at Gallaudet University, where I taught interpretation from 1984 to 2000. I am now the Director of Curriculum and Instruction for the Effective Interpreting Professional Education Series at Language Matters, Inc. (LMI). I continue to focus on developing interpreter education materials and providing up-to-date training for interpreters and interpreter educators.

See www.language_matters.com for additional information on courses offered by Language Matters that address the topics in *The Effective Interpreting Series*. LMI also offers graduate level courses on teaching interpreting.

The exercises presented in this book result from my desire to develop materials that practicing and future interpreters can use in or out of the classroom while studying simultaneous interpretation. This book can be used independently of any other book in *The Effective Interpreting Series,* or it can be used as one of the sequence of five books that provide a systematic approach to developing skills in simultaneous interpreting from English to any other language.

In my experience I have found that one of the greatest challenges in interpreter education for signed or spoken language is finding or creating appropriate materials for use in the classroom. An even more severe problem is overcoming the lack of study materials that practicing and future interpreters can use on their own, either for refresher practice or for continuing professional development. There is a growing demand for mentorship in both signed and spoken language interpretation and materials to optimize these contacts.

Simultaneous interpreting is a very complex skill that requires intensive and appropriate practice. It is my hope that by providing materials for developing simultaneous interpreting skills from English to any other language, practicing and future interpreters will find the process of developing interpretation skills to be rewarding and effective.

Successful interpreters rely on many skills in their everyday work. The development of these skills is not intuitive or automatic. Simultaneous interpreting must be developed through a careful sequence of learning activities. Isolating specific skills and learning them one at a time is the best approach to learning complex new skills. Learning new skills one at a time allows the mastery of individual skills and a feeling of success. Gaining control over components of the interpretation process can assist in developing simultaneous interpreting skills because appropriate practice helps to routinize these complex skills. The skills that make up the simultaneous interpreting processes are generally not used in isolation and must be synthesized correctly in order to render an interpretation.

Component skills for simultaneous interpreting are interactive and interdependent. The learning process should begin with strengthening skills in your first language (L1) and move in a carefully structured sequence from *intra*lingual skill development to *inter*lingual development. The first four volumes in *The Effective Interpreting Series* provide English source materials and exercises that focus on cognitive processing, English skills development, translation, and consecutive interpreting. This volume provides practice materials designed to develop simultaneous interpreting skills from English to any other language.

Description of the Materials

The Effective Interpreting Series: Simultaneous Interpreting from English consists of a study set with a workbook and videotext. Ideally, these materials follow *Cognitive Processing in English, English Skills Development, Translating from English,* and *Consecutive Interpreting from English.* The study set refers to the exercises on the videotext. In the upper right corner of the videotext you will see the unit and exercise number. For example, Ex. 1.2 is the second exercise in Unit 1. The following topics are included in this volume: consecutive interpreting, bridging to simultaneous, sources of error, comprehension, transfer, memory, reformulation, and self-monitoring and correction. The exercise materials progress from easy to more difficult within each unit. As you move through the text some of the exercises provide a review from previous volumes of *The Effective Interpreting Series.*

How to Use This Book

What You Need before Beginning the Exercises

You need specific equipment in order to get the maximum benefit from these exercises. Here is what you will need in addition to the video and book: a VHS VCR with a remote control that allows you to pause the video, a TV monitor, a video camera, a supply of blank videotapes on which you can record your interpretations, an audio recorder, blank audiotapes, and a quiet place to work.

If you are working into a signed language, having easy access to a video camera enhances the study process. If you are working into a signed language, it is best to have your work videotaped in picture-in-picture format so that the source and the target languages are available on the same videotape. If you do not have picture-in-picture capability, a video camera focusing on you (and the speaker if possible) while you are interpreting will allow you to record the auditory source language and visual target simultaneously. This is not ideal but will allow you to have source and target on the same videotape. Spoken language interpreters working without a camera will need a tape recorder to record the spoken interpretation. Be sure that your tape recorder is close enough to the video source so that your audiotape records the sound from the English source tape and your voice.

When and Where You Should Plan to Do the Exercises

Each exercise can be done on your own. If you are using these materials in a classroom environment, your teacher will assign some exercises for out of class and may use the first exercise in each unit as a group exercise or warm up. Where you do the exercises will depend on your instructor and the equipment available in your interpreter education program. For example, if your instructional program has a language lab that will permit you to work independently and to record your work, then you can do many of the exercises independently while on campus or in class. Your teacher may introduce the exercises and go over your results with you.

If you are a practicing interpreter and want to work on your skills for professional development you will still need all of the equipment listed previously and may proceed at your own pace. You may wish to form a study group to have a forum to discuss your skill-development work, both product and process.

How Many Times Should You Do the Exercises

You can benefit from doing each exercise at least twice. When you do the exercise the first time, the material and skills may be new and unfamiliar. When you do the exercise the second time, the material will be "warm," or familiar, because you have read and heard it once and have tried the exercise once. If you are already a simultaneous interpreter you may still find some of the exercise difficult because focusing attention on specific component skills is different than the cognitive challenge of simultaneous interpreting. The skills you practice will become more familiar and automatic. Automaticity improves control of the processes you use to create the product.

Five-Step Follow-Up

The purpose of the follow-up is to introduce and strengthen the concepts of self-assessment and insight into the process of interpreting. Interpreters who have accurate self-assessment skills can enjoy lifelong learning and continuing education opportunities in a wide variety of settings, even if a teacher or mentor is not available. Self-assessment skills lead to accountability in interpretation because they allow you to analyze both the process and the product of your work. Accountability means that you make conscious decisions about both the processes involved and the products achieved in your work, increasing the ability to faithfully interpret the original message. Accountability also means that you take responsibility when the interpretation is not faithful to the message and correct it.

By carefully doing each follow-up, you will learn the importance of the many components of the interpreting process and see that each component is needed for a successful interpretation. Separating simultaneous interpreting into its component parts and processes allows you to understand where to focus your efforts for improvement.

A graduate of the Master of Arts in Interpretation at Gallaudet who became very familiar with the follow-up suggests that the impact of self-assessment available through the follow-up is unparalleled (Fleetwood, 1998, personal communication).

The five-step follow-up is presented after the study questions in most of the exercises and is explained below.

The five-step follow-up has a different format in *Simultaneous Interpreting from English* than it did in the earlier volumes of *The Effective Interpreting Series.* The five-step follow-up now allows you to examine your interpretation carefully, determine which part of the process may have negatively affected the product, and make revisions. The follow-up also allows you to determine the effect of errors on the communicative event. It is important to keep in mind that the participants that you envision in preparing to render your interpretation are the ones who will be affected by the errors.

Doing the Follow-Up

Review your entire interpretation. Select the portion that you would like to analyze and revise (this part will vary in length from 1 to 3 minutes). You will analyze only this portion of your work. You will use the steps below to revise each error that you identify.

List at least one positive aspect of your interpretation.

Examples:

Maintained composure

Clear pronunciation

Step 1 **Interpretation Rendered**

Transcribe only the portion of the interpretation you would like to improve. You do not need to transcribe the source text. Write only the portion of the interpretation that needs revision. This should be a phrase rather than a single word. If you are working into a signed language, use capital letters and gloss only the portion you would like to revise. Glossing is a system that allows linguists to note the features of a sign language utterance so that the utterance can be studied carefully. For our purposes we will not be using a full system of glossing. Instead, use capital letters to write the name of the sign to which you are referring. A brief description of glossing is provided in the terminology section of this workbook.

This example uses English as the target language. The original message is, "John found his keys." If part of your interpretation does not accurately convey the message, write down that part.

"John lost his keys."

Step 2 **Determine Underlying Reason**

Although there are many possible reasons for errors in interpretation, in this analysis you will select one of the following for each error identified in Step 1.

Comprehension

Transfer

Reformulation

For this example we assume that the interpreter did not understand the source message correctly and select comprehension as the underlying reason.

Step 3 **Probable Effect of Error on Communicative Function**

After selecting the type of error, rate the error according to how it impacts the communication, keeping in mind that not all errors are equally serious. In

English Skills Development and *Cognitive Processing in English,* the emphasis was on finding the reasons for the errors. According to Kussmaul (1995), finding reasons for errors is appropriate for language learning, but in interpreting it is more relevant to determine the *communicative function* of the error. For example, does the error distort the message or is there a "sufficient degree of precision"? In this step you will select from the choices below in determining the probable effect of errors on the communicative function of your interpretation. Remember that you will develop your interpretations with an audience in mind.

5 = No negative consequences to participants

4 = Consequence of errors is minimal

3 = Consequence of errors is moderate

2 = Consequence of errors is severe

1 = Consequence of errors is grave

Since the interpretation conveys the opposite meaning of that intended by the source message, the probable effect of the error is likely severe and could be grave depending on the context in which this occurred.

Step 4 **Revisions**

Write, and then later record, a revised interpretation that better preserves the meaning of the original source message.

"John found his keys."

Step 5 **Action Plan for Improvement**

Once you have determined the type of error and its impact, write down what action you plan to take to improve your work. For example, you can decide to focus on comprehension and review the material until you are certain you have fully understood the message, or you can re-record your interpretation to create an improved product.

If you find difficulties in transferring the message across language boundaries, you may wish to study the concepts presented in *Translating from English.* If you need new source material for translation practice, you may use any of the source materials in the other four volumes of *The Effective Interpreting Series.*

By carefully doing each follow-up, you will learn the importance of the many components of the interpreting process and see that each component is needed for a successful interpretation. Separating interpreting into its component parts and processes allows you to understand where to focus your efforts for improvement and builds automaticity. More importantly, the follow-up helps you to understand the impact of errors on communication. For example, background noise may be a part of the communicative event over which you do not have control, but you may be able to build cognitive strategies that allow you to avoid being distracted by the noise.

The follow-up should be completed as soon as possible after finishing the exercises. You will be able to explain your reasoning more easily when the follow-up process is done soon after the exercises. An example of the five-step follow-up is given on page 116. using a hypothetical student named Pat who has just completed the exercises in Unit 3. There is no follow-up in Units 1 and 2.

Progress Tracking Sheet

A progress tracking sheet is at the end of each unit. This sheet is designed to help you keep track of which exercises you have completed and your performance on these exercises. After completing the exercise, answering the study questions, and doing the follow-up, fill in the tracking sheet. Note the date that you completed the exercise and give an indication of your level of accomplishment. You can use either a quantitative or a qualitative approach to track your progress. The sample chart that follows provides examples of how to note your progress using the quantitative or qualitative approach.

A quantitative approach uses a point scale. Assigning points to linguistic exercises is arbitrary and difficult to do. Nevertheless, in academic environments you may find the point system more common than the qualitative approach. Each of the two trials on the performance and each study question and follow-up step can be assigned a point value. For example, a zero indicates that the question was not answered and a 5 indicates a full and complete response. Add the scores in each column (not row) and divide by the number of exercises to get a percentage for first performance, second performance, study questions, and follow-up. It is important to have separate percentages for each of these columns because the scores in the study question and follow-up columns represent different skills. The two performance columns measure how you actually did on the exercise. A second trial on the same material is considered practice on warm or familiar material and should be weighted less than the "cold" or first attempt to interpret the selection.

Here is an example of a scale you can use to assign points to your work. Excellent (no serious errors) = 5 points; good (some errors, but not serious) = 4 points; fair (many errors, some serious) = 3 points; not satisfactory = 2 points (many errors, most are serious); poor =1 point (missed the point of the exercise—must redo).

A qualitative approach is well suited to those who are studying the material in an independent fashion or those who do not want to attach numbers and percentages to their work. In a qualitative approach you describe your response to your work rather than assigning numbers. Write down enough information to remind yourself of your level of achievement in the performance of the exercises, study questions, and follow-up.

Your teacher may ask you to photocopy this page and submit it for grading.

Exercise Number	Date	First Performance	Study Questions	Follow-up Activity	Questions and Reminders	Date	Second Performance
Exercise 3.1 Quantitative	9/9					9/10	
Qualitative		Missed about 50% of message	Complete	Did not do	Stess level is high; try to relax		Struggling to keep up
Exercise 3.2 Quantitative	9/14					9/16	
Qualitative		Hard to keep up	Rating shows stress is high	Gained insight	Practice more with this type of material		Much improved
Exercise 3.3 Quantitative							
Qualitative							
Quantitative Totals							

Introduction to Simultaneous Interpreting

Goal of This Book and Video

The goal of this study set is to provide you with a systematically arranged set of experiences that develop skill in simultaneous interpreting of English monologic source materials. The book does not attempt to provide a complete review of the literature on simultaneous interpretation, but rather selects key aspects of the simultaneous interpreting process, presents relevant theoretical aspects of those processes, and provides exercises that relate to those points.

Although consecutive and simultaneous interpreting share some cognitive abilities, there are also important distinctions between these two skills and the processes that underlie each. Certain topics that first appeared in both *Consecutive Interpreting from English* and other volumes of *The Effective Interpreting Series* have been adapted here to serve as stepping stones toward simultaneous interpreting.

In each unit, a brief introduction provides theoretical background information on the unit's topic and discusses the relevance of that information to simultaneous interpretation. The introductory material is followed by exercises specifically designed to apply the theoretical concepts discussed in that unit. In turn, each exercise has three parts. One part is to respond to the exercise material and record your answers. This allows you to create a product. Second, answering the study questions allows you to examine your product and consider theoretical aspects of your work. The third aspect of each exercise is the follow-up. The follow-up allows you to determine underlying reasons for the error and the communicative impact of your interpretation and make plans for improvement.

The exercises in each unit are based on the videotext. The texts are unrehearsed examples of spoken English. Some speakers prepared their remarks in advance and some spoke extemporaneously. All of the speakers are native speakers of English. One speaker is originally from England and her accent reflects that. None of the speakers read their presentations. Seleskovitch and Lederer (1995) stress the importance of practicing with authentic spoken materials. Unrehearsed spoken materials have naturally occurring hesitations, pauses, and repetitions. In the book, the spoken material is transcribed to make English available in written form. Although English that is spoken and later transcribed is different in form than English that is initially created in a written format, the transcript of the spoken English simply provides a more accessible way to analyze and discuss aspects of the source message. When practicing with this material you should work from the spoken version, not the written version.

The exercises in this book progress from easy to more difficult. The first unit focuses on error types. The remaining units focus on specific aspects of the simultaneous interpreting process.

You should plan to videotape all of your interpretations. The recording is an accurate record of your interpretation and allows you to clearly see your strengths and weaknesses. Videotaping your work also allows you to see yourself as your future audience or clients will see you. "The audience's impression is clearly influenced by both the verbal and non-verbal behavior (of the interpreter). If the interpreter speaks haltingly or appears unsure, the credibility of his/her interpreting will be diminished" (Kurz, 2002, p.79).

All of the exercises (recording, answering the study questions, and the follow-up) in each unit may be completed as out-of-classroom work or as independent work during class time, if appropriate equipment is available. This book provides complete directions for each exercise. The directions guide you to the correct location on the accompanying videotext. In the upper right corner of the videotext you will see the unit and exercise number. For example, Ex. 1.2 is the second exercise in Unit 1.

Performing the exercises in this book provides structured and intensive practice in the components of simultaneous interpreting. This type of practice allows you to synthesize the various processes within simultaneous interpreting. These study materials stand apart from existing materials because they include videotaped source texts that are carefully keyed to this book. The book contains exercises that are designed to help you routinize the sub-skills needed for effective interpreting. The more you practice the sub-skills of interpreting, the more likely you will be able to effectively handle the synthesis of the interpreting components necessary for effective simultaneous interpreting.

If you are beyond the beginning stages of an interpreter education program or are already a practicing interpreter, you can benefit from practicing simultaneous interpreting skills, either as a refresher course or for professional skill maintenance. According to Ericsson (2001, p. 189) in his discussions of expertise, individuals who have already achieved levels of success as professionals can improve their performance, if motivated to do so, through additional training and deliberate practice.

Interpreters sometimes experience the "plateau effect" in training. The plateau effect occurs when skills appear to no longer develop as rapidly as they did earlier in the training process. This is a common occurrence. When progress seems to stagnate, it is often useful to go back to an earlier stage of skill development and practice at that level. Taking time to go back and review skills is a positive step because it increases confidence, builds mastery, and often provides the springboard to further progress. If your simultaneous interpreting skills are at a plateau, you may find it useful to spend some time working on the various sub-skills highlighted in other volumes of *The Effective Interpreting Series.*

At the end of each unit there is a progress tracking sheet. Use the progress tracking sheet to note the date you completed the exercises and to make notes regarding your progress as well as to record any questions you may have about the exercise. The tracking sheet can be used in either a quantitative or a qualitative approach.

The History of Simultaneous Interpreting

In 1945 the trials for the surviving Nazi war criminals began. The trials were held in Nuremberg and have since been called the Nuremberg trials. These trials mark the beginning of the profession of simultaneous interpreting because prior to 1945 almost all interpreting was done in consecutive mode. The four working languages of the trials were German, English, French, and Russian. According to Ramler (1988), using consecutive interpreting would have caused the trials to last more than four years.

Ramler described the working conditions of the simultaneous interpreters. There were four booths, with three interpreters in each. In the English booth one interpreter would work from Russian into English, another from German into English, and the third from French into English. The interpreters working at the Nuremberg trials had to select a team of interpreters to work with, devise equipment, and set up working practices. They had no criteria or standards to follow, but rather relied on intuition and experience. They realized quickly that preparation was important, especially given the nature of the testimony they were likely to hear. They also realized that their voices and personalities could affect the message. The interpreters who worked at the Nuremberg trials were the pioneers who assisted the profession in the transition from consecutive to simultaneous interpreting.

Interpreting Research

Gile (1994a, p. 149–152) summarized the history of simultaneous interpreting research. In the 1950s most "research" was based on interpreters attempting to explain the complex process of simultaneous interpreting by reflecting on their own personal experiences. In the 1960s and 1970s researchers began to develop hypotheses about the interpreting process and test them. During the late 1970s and 1980s several models of interpreting were developed. In the 1980s, 1990s, and up to the present we find many more studies on interpretation. Riccardi (2002a) points out that, according to Pochhacker (1995), the number of research works dealing with interpretation between 1952 and 1988 was double that of the 36 years that preceded this 6-year span. The relatively young discipline of interpretation studies has demanded an increasing amount of attention from researchers.

Although current research in interpretation allows exploration of various aspects of interpretation, this section focuses on quality, expertise, and evaluation. These topics are integrally related. Studies on quality and expertise point to types of performances and strategies that yield successful interpretations. Contrasting successful and less successful interpretations allows a more empirical base for evaluation of interpretations.

Interpretation Quality

Kalina (2002) reviews the literature on interpretation quality and points out that the early works of Seleskovitch and others focus on "conveying sense, not wording." But "...quality cannot be determined simply on the basis of sense predominating over words. It is equally inappropriate to judge simultaneous interpreting in relation to quantitative indices such as decalage" (p. 121). Kalina explains that early in interpretation research quality was judged by comparing source and target language transcriptions and that one of the main flaws in this approach is that it does not take the environmental factors that affect the interpreter and interpretation into account. Kalina points out that quality is likely to deteriorate when one of the three main efforts in Gile's model demands extra processing capacity than is available, affecting the overall quality of the interpretation.

Kalina says that sometimes quality in interpretation is determined by examining the product (Pochhacker, 1994). In this view, the target text is evaluated independently of the source message. In contrast, "Moser-Mercer (1994a, p. 44) identifies, as the optimum quality goal, a complete, accurate, undistorted rendition of the original, taking into account extra-linguistic information subject to situational constraints" (Kalina, 2002, p. 123).

There are various perspectives and relationships to consider in judging quality in interpretation. Kalina (2002) says that the relationships among speakers, interpreters, source and target texts, and users all can be considered. Interpreters who consistently demonstrate high levels of quality also possess other characteristics that describe expertise. A summary of Ericsson's (2001) study on expertise and how it relates to interpreting follows.

Interpreting Expertise

Before discussing expertise in interpreting we must know what expertise itself means. "Expert performers can reliably reproduce their performance any time when required such as during competition and training" (Ericsson, 2001, p. 192). An expert can usually function with reliable accuracy. Ericsson's work suggests that expertise in various domains is acquired through interaction with specific training activities and deliberate practice.

If we know which activities related to the interpreting process provide appropriate practice, we can develop more effective study and practice habits.

Ericsson and Smith (1991) suggest that it is possible to devise tasks that characterize expertise and that this can be accomplished for most domains. The activities and practice methods in the chapters that follow are designed to provide access to activities that can lead to expertise in interpreting. It is important to practice on appropriate materials because, as Bloom (1985) suggests, access to the best training resources is necessary to reach the highest levels of expertise. In other words, the practice must be related to the domain in which one wishes to improve. This is more fully explained below.

Ericsson (2001, p.192) provides several claims about expertise that generalize across domains when seeking to measure the "superior reproducible performance of experts that can be measured during development" (Ericsson, 1996).

1. "The level of achievement increases gradually, there are no abrupt improvements in performance."
2. "The age at which experts typically reach their peak career performance is the middle to late 20s for many vigorous sports and a decade later for arts and sciences."
3. "The most compelling evidence for the requirement of engagement in domain related activities prior to attaining high levels of performance that even the most talented need around ten years of intense involvement before they reach international level in sports, sciences, and the arts" (Ericsson et al., 1993).

Hoffman (1997) cites Moser-Mercer, who says, "It could take between six to ten years on the job to become recognized as a real expert in conference interpreting" (p. 198). Hoffman (1997) suggests that novices move through levels or predictable stages and says, a. The development of expertise involves a progression from a superficial and literal understanding of problems to an articulated, conceptual, and principled understanding. b. Over the course of development it is rare for a level to be skipped; it is rare for a proficient practitioner to either regress or fail to progress unless they fall out of practice. c. With practice a skill loses the quality of being conscious, effortful, deliberate, and linear, and takes on the patter of automatic pattern recognition. d. When teaching others, the proficient practitioner can anticipate the errors a trainee will make and can do so in a way that takes into account each trainee's skill level" (p. 198).

If we apply these notions to interpreter training, we can see that gradual improvement over time is a natural unfolding of skill and that the higher levels of skill will be more apparent after years of practice. It is realistic to expect that skills will improve over time, rather than be at peak levels at the conclusion of training. This fact lends support to the idea that entry level interpreters need mentorship and guidance over time in order to fully develop their skills. However, it is possible to maximize the effect of contact with interpreter training curricula. Hoffman (1997) suggests that practice that simulates real-world requirements is one way to develop expertise while in training. It is likely that specific types of practice can move a motivated person toward expertise more quickly than exercises that are not related to specific goals.

In order to find out what activities should be practiced, Ericsson et al. (1993) identified the training activities most closely associated with optimal improvement of performance and classified them as effective, deliberate practice.

Characteristics of Effective Practice

If practice is the avenue to developing expertise for beginners or more experienced interpreters, it is important to know what kinds of practice will be helpful and how long practice should last. Ericsson's (2001) work focuses on the importance of *effective* practice and says, "Improvement of performance was uniformly observed when individuals, who were motivated to improve their performance, were given well-defined tasks, were provided with feedback, and had ample opportunities for repetition. Individuals were able to keep improving during a series of training sessions as long as the sessions were limited to around an hour—the time college students were able to maintain sufficient concentration to make active efforts to improve" (p. 193).

Ericsson (2001) also emphasizes the importance of *deliberate* practice and notes that "Deliberate efforts include problem solving and finding better methods to perform the tasks" (p. 193). Deliberate practice on appropriate materials is important for improving performance. According to Ericsson (2001, p.194), the main characteristics of deliberate practice are solitary practice with full concentration and the intention to improve certain aspects of performance. For musicians who practiced in this way there were consistent correlations between the level of attained performance and the amount and quality of solitary activities. To emphasize the importance of the amount of time spent in solitary practice, Ericsson et al. (1993) compared three groups of musicians. The most accomplished musicians had practiced for about 10,000 hours by age 20. Two other groups of musicians who had practiced 5,000 and 2,500 hours, respectively, were ranked second and third in skill compared to the group who had practiced 10,000 hours.

Deliberate practice is important for attaining high levels of skill and also for maintaining expertise. The concept of deliberate practice also accounts for individual differences in the maintenance of expert performance (p. 194 in Ericsson, 2001). Those who continue in deliberate solitary practice are likely to maintain their expertise.

Self-Confidence

Not only do experts exhibit reliably reproducible performances, but also they tend to have identifiable personality characteristics. Keiser (1978) says that experts have good communication skills and can convince others of their expertise and that these characteristics are a good basis for interpreting expertise. Hoffman (1997) summarizes research on expertise and notes that experts show self-confidence (Bradley, 1981) and are willing to stand behind their decisions (Klemp and McClelland, 1986). Hoffman suggests that interpreting students who do not have self-confidence generally do not progress as well as those who do.

Through deliberate, effective practice you can improve your interpreting skills in a systematic way. Knowing that you are taking these steps helps to improve your overall self-confidence and can lead to greater expertise.

Terminology

Terms and concepts associated with simultaneous interpreting needed to use the study set are summarized below.

An Interpretation

Following Bell's (1991) distinctions, an interpretation is the product of the process of interpreting, or the target text. An interpretation should accurately reproduce the grammatical and lexical features as well as the style and content of the source text.

Consecutive Interpreting

According to Gonzalez et al. (1991, p. 379), "In consecutive interpreting the interpreter waits until the speaker has finished the source language message before rendering the message into the target language. The duration of the source language may be anywhere from a few seconds to several minutes." There are two types of consecutive interpreting: short consecutive and long consecutive.

- **Short consecutive**

Short consecutive is the term used to describe interpretation of short segments of discourse, such as a sentence or a few sentences.

- **Long consecutive**

Long consecutive is the term used to describe interpretation of more lengthy passages, such as several paragraphs or possibly an entire speech.

Gloss

"Glosses provide a convenient way to use one language to reference another. Specifically, a gloss is a symbol or group of symbols in one language representing the core meaning of a particular symbol or symbol group from another language. Glosses do not present translations or interpretations and, thus, do not represent natural language use" (Fleetwood, 1998, personal communication).

Students working between ASL and English will use written English words to *represent* the meanings of ASL signs. A complete glossing system would include non-manual signals as well as information that indicates which sign is meant. In this study set, you do not need to fill in the non-manual signals unless you are already familiar with such a system. It is very important to realize that there is not a one-to-one correspondence between ASL signs and glosses used to represent the signs.

When people see an English word used as a gloss, many become confused about the difference among the gloss, the ASL sign that it references, and the English word as it is used in natural interaction. This confusion sometimes leads people who have little familiarity with ASL to think that ASL is a form of English. It is not. The glosses are an invented convention to allow us to make a note about which sign we intend to use.

Linguists use glosses when they study ASL and need to transcribe the signs they are looking at into a written form. A gloss is usually written in capital letters. For example, the ASL gloss for the English word "bike," is BIKE. This does not mean that there is always a one-to-one correspondence between ASL signs and English words. BIKE could also be used as the gloss for the English word "bicycle". The English word "run" has many possible glosses in ASL, including DRIP, UNRAVEL, and COMPETE.

It is not necessary to develop a complete and complicated glossing system in order to do the exercises in this study set. Instead, jot down the gloss for the sign as best you can and use that in your follow-up. The gloss will help you remember how you want to sign your interpretation. Remember that a gloss is simply a reference to a core meaning. It is not intended as a natural interpretation.

Illocutionary Force

The illocutionary force of a message conveys the intent or mood of the speaker. Larson (1984) says that the form of the message reveals the illocutionary force. For example, if the utterance is in the form of a command, it has a different meaning than if it is in the form of a question. The word "Go!" has a different meaning than the word "Go?" The three broad categories of statements, commands, or questions include most examples of illocutionary force.

Interpreting

Interpreting is the *process* or activity involved in transferring a message from one language to another in real time. The message is usually spoken rather than written. A feature that distinguishes translation from interpretation is that the interpreter is part of the communication dynamic. Seleskovitch (1978a) suggests that the very presence of the interpreter within the communicative event is the major difference between interpretation and translation. According to Gonzalez et al. (1991), interpreting is the oral form of the translation process. "Interpreters must instantaneously arrive at a target language equivalent, while at the same time searching for further input" (Gonzalez et al., 1991, p. 295).

Process and Product

In interpreter education there is much discussion over whether you should focus on the process of the interpretation or the product of the interpretation.

Both are important and you should be aware of them even during the earliest stages of your training. It is vital that you understand the difference between these two terms and the role they play in your education and training. The process of interpretation is largely invisible. The process is what goes on in your head as you listen, analyze, and transfer the meaning from one language to another. The product, the message rendered in the target language, is the observable result of the process.

The processes associated with interpretation cannot be recorded or observed by another person. Only via retrospection can the interpreter gain insight into his or her own process. This insight can lead to changed strategies and better control of the interpreting process. Gile (1995) suggests that adopting a process-oriented approach can optimize training time. In Gile's opinion it is best not to focus only on the end products of the process, but rather to include information on "principles, methods and procedures" (p.10). Gile says, "By concentrating on the reasons for errors or good choices rather than on the words or structures produced by the students, teachers devote most of their effective teaching time to strategies and lose little time over their by-products" (p.11). Gile goes on to say that later on in interpreter training programs, additional emphasis must be placed on the product, but only after the underlying processes are established.

The product is the observable part of your work. It is the message in the target language that the audience receives from the sender via your interpretation. The product can be recorded for future analysis, while the process cannot. Seal (1999, p. 14) summarized the results of a recent study of sign language interpreters who wished to improve their skills. In that report, she emphasizes the importance of analyzing one's own work. "Self-analysis, the zenith of any professional development activity, is highly facilitated when we step back and take a look at ourselves. Routine videotaping and observing videotaped performances for strengths and weaknesses and for change over time is quite possibly the most valuable, yet least frequently accomplished activity we can engage in." For sign language interpreters, videotaping allows you to review the product. Spoken language interpreters can review their work on audiotape.

Simultaneous Interpreting

Gonzalez et al. (1991, p. 359) say that simultaneous interpreting is the process wherein the interpreter speaks at the same time as the source language speaker. In this process the source language is rendered into the target language while the source is ongoing. The term "simultaneous interpreting" is really a misnomer because there is always at least a slight time differential between the time the original message is spoken and when the interpretation is delivered.

Simply stated, simultaneous interpreting is a procedure by which the interpreter listens to a message and concurrently reorganizes the information into linguistic structures that are appropriate for the target language. Simultaneous interpretation is one type of language transfer that begins while the source message is ongoing. The length of the interpretation depends on the length of the source message. It can vary from a single utterance to an entire speech.

Source Language

This is the language you are translating or interpreting *from.*

Target Language

This is the language you are working *into.* This is sometimes called the receptor language.

Translating

According to Bell (1991, p.13), translating is the *process* of or activity involved in transferring a message from one language to another. An important characteristic of translation is that the source and target messages can be re-examined, whether they are in print or on videotape, since the transfer is not done in real time.

Models of Interpretation

Although there are many models of interpretation, for brevity's sake only three are summarized here. These models refer to spoken language but can be applied to signed language interpreting as well.

Seleskovitch

Niska (1999) summarizes Seleskovitch's theory of the interpretation process. "The main idea behind the theory put forth by Seleskovitch and Lederer is that interpreting is based on meaning (Fr. "sens"), not on words or linguistic structures, and it has therefore become known as the théorie du sens. In this theory, it is assumed that the spoken original (in chunks of 7–8 words) is retained in short-term memory for only a few seconds, after which cognitive complements at work on these words transform them into meaning units. As soon as these meaning units are formed, they melt in turn into larger meaning units (Seleskovitch & Lederer 1989, p. 247). The model postulates that there exists a) an immediate short-time memory working on predominantly phonological input with a capacity of 7–8 words which are saved for 2-3 seconds; b) a cognitive short-time memory that forms the base for a semantic memory.

The interpreting process thus consists of three phases:

1. Verbal phase—incoming discourse
2. Non-verbal phase—processing
3. Verbal phase—reproduction of the message

In the non-verbal phase the verbal input (phase 1) is split into meaning units which melt together with previous knowledge (subject specific or general knowledge) and enters the cognitive memory, thereby losing their verbal form by transforming into ideas."

Moser-Mercer

Some models of simultaneous interpretation include diagrams to represent the possible stages in the process and relationships among the stages. Other models are more general in approach and describe the main stages in the process. In looking at either a detailed or a global model, it is important to remember that each model represents a theoretical opinion about what happens in the interpretation process. Models can be useful when studying interpretation because models help break down a complex process into smaller pieces that can be studied and mastered. No data have been reported that support the notion that studying a model of interpretation actually improves interpreting performance for beginners, although it may.

Moser-Mercer suggests that even though most researchers agree that interpretation is a multistage process, they do not agree on the names of the stages or the contents of the stages. Moser-Mercer concludes that "A powerful model of the interpreting process must be broad enough to include aspects that reflect the complex, time constrained multitasking environment of simultaneous interpreting that involves a high degree of cognitive processing" (Moser-Mercer , 1997, p. 194). For detailed information on the models Moser-Mercer refers to, please see the chapter by Moser-Mercer in Danks et *al.* (1997). Models of interpretation describe the ideal path that the interpretation process can follow. Some models of interpretation attempt to describe what happens in the interpreter's mind during interpretation (process), while other models describe the observable portion of the interpretation (product).

Gile

Gile suggests that since interpreting is fundamentally so difficult, studying models may help the interpreter select and develop effective interpreting strategies. Gile's Effort Model is one that he has developed over time and is based on his own research and research in cognitive psychology. The model is based on two basic principles.

- "Interpretation requires mental energy that is only available in limited supply."
- "Interpretation takes up almost all of this mental energy, and sometimes requires more than is available, at which times performance deteriorates." (p. 161)

Gile explains that some mental operations are nonautomatic and require attention, while automatic operations do not. "Non automatic operations take processing capacity from a limited available supply." This understanding led to the development of a model that acknowledges that there are certain cognitive requirements and capacity limitations during the interpreting process. Gile (2001) says that simultaneous interpreting consists of "concurrent operations each of which requires processing capacity (PC), and the amount of PC required is often as much as—or even more than the interpreter has available at the same time it is needed" (p. 2). The "efforts" Gile describes can be grouped as three efforts.

- The listening effort includes listening to and analyzing the source message.
- The production effort includes producing a message in the target language.
- The short-term memory effort includes efforts to store information until it can be rendered into the target language.

Gile describes the differences between consecutive and simultaneous this way. "In *simultaneous, two languages are processed at the same time* in 'working memory' (roughly, the cognitive resources engaged in short-term processing of information just received). This requires devoting some attention to inhibiting the influence of the source language when producing the target language speech in order to avoid interference. In consecutive this constraint is much weaker, or even non-existent, depending on the way the notes are taken (even if notes are taken in the source language, they are generally single words, rather than full sentence structures, hence the likelihood of less interference). Moreover, while speaking, the interpreter can devote more attention to monitoring his/her output in consecutive than in simultaneous as part of the Production Effort."

Gile also says "In simultaneous, target-speech production occurs under heavier time pressure than in consecutive, where the interpreter can pace him/herself. This is particularly important for speech segments with high information density, where the pressure in simultaneous is particularly high. In consecutive, it is also high during the listening phase and therefore affects Note Production, but loses its urgency during the reformulation phase."

Being aware of the aspects and phases of interpretation can help you focus your available capacities on the tasks that need your immediate attention during the process. Gile explains that when the requirements of the tasks exceed your current capacity, problems are triggered that can lead to failures in interpretation. As an example of the overwhelming amount of information that the human mind processes, Gonzalez et al. (1991) point out that Wortman et al. (1988) estimated that "in each second our senses receive 100 million pieces of information and can also accommodate numerous sources of stimuli simultaneously" (p. 351).

Competencies in Interpreting

There are specific competencies that must be in place before beginning simultaneous interpreting (Gonzalez et al., 1991, p. 346, Roberts, 1995, p. 37). Some of these competencies are described below. The competencies fall into six broad categories: linguistic, cognitive, methodological, cultural, content, and interpersonal competencies. These are important in any interpreting situation. In addition to these, the interpreter should be an expert in interpreting. The interpreter must be linguistically adept, cognitively able to manage several tasks at once, be knowledgeable about both cultures and the content of the material, and have interpersonal skills that facilitate natural interaction among the participants in the communicative setting.

Linguistic Competencies

Linguistic competency includes language proficiency, transfer competency, and methodological competencies. Interpreters must have high levels of language proficiency that allows understanding of the source language and its nuances as well as the ability to express oneself correctly, fluently, clearly, and with poise in the target language (Roberts, 1995).

Word Recognition Skills

One example of language proficiency is word recognition skills. De Groot (2000) addresses the importance of word recognition skills as an area that may have been overlooked in interpreter training. Well-developed word recognition skills can become nearly automatic, which saves cognitive energy for more complex tasks. DeGroot suggests, "The solution is to automatize word recognition as much as possible through training. When the stage of maximal automaticity of word recognition is reached, all resources can be directed to those components of the task that defy automatization" (p.55). For example, when you read a new word for the first time, you use more cognitive effort than when you read a word that you already know.

DeGroot's comments about automatitzing word recognition skills are especially relevant to fingerspelled word recognition in signed language interpreting. Failure to recognize fingerspelled words in context on the first try is the single greatest difficulty for signed language interpreters (Patrie, 1988). Word recognition failures, whether the words are fingerspelled or signed, are likely to account for a large percentage of errors in signed language interpreting from ASL to English or complete breakdowns in the interpreting process. These errors are due to lack of specific training on fingerspelled word recognition and to a lack of training in ASL comprehension, either of which could lead to problems in automaticity. The importance of visual word recognition skills extends to correctly recognizing signs in context for signed language interpreters. For spoken language interpreters the challenge is to recognize spoken words in context.

DeGroot goes on to explain that auditory word recognition could also benefit from direct training because the spoken signal can often be accompanied by interfering noises from the environment or poor speech patterns. Second, spoken words vanish as they are spoken and cannot be re-inspected as a printed word can. DeGroot suggests that when direct training on word recognition is automatized more cognitive resources are left for two other important aspects of interpreting. The two other aspects are as follows: (1) parts of the process that cannot be automatized (figuring out which meaning is intended) and (2) temporary storage of information. These two aspects compete with each other for cognitive processing allocations. When more effort is needed for one, there is less resource for the other. So it makes good sense to automatize as many sub-processes as you can.

Transfer Competence

Transfer competence is a form of linguistic competence that allows the interpreter to understand the message in one language and express it in another. Roberts (1995) suggests that transfer competence involves more than understanding the gist of the original message. "Transfer competence includes the ability to understand the articulation of meaning in the source language discourse and the ability to render the meaning of the source language discourse in the target language accurately. Transfer competence also includes the ability to transfer a message from a source language into a target language without undue influence of the source language as well as the ability to transfer a message from a source language into a target language appropriately from the point of view of style."

Cognitive Flexibility Competence

Competence in cognitive flexibility assumes that all of the other linguistic competencies are in place and that the interpreter can rapidly access the competencies as needed during the interpretation process. For specific skill-building exercises in comprehension, memory, acuity and discrimination, immediate repetition, delayed repetition, number repetition, word level pattern inference, phrase level pattern inference, and multi-tasking please see *The Effective Interpreting Series: Cognitive Processing in English.*

• Control of attention

Control of attention is one aspect of cognitive processing. After practicing the sub-components of the interpreting process, you must develop control of attention. The interpreter must coordinate the many cognitive tasks involved in simultaneous interpreting. Gile (1995) describes this as the "coordination effort." De Groot (2000) summarizes related research to show that the coordination effort can and should be treated separately in interpreter training. DeGroot explains that Gopher et al. (1988) studied attention strategies of subjects who trained to play a complex computer game. Some subjects practiced playing the game without specific instruction while other subjects had training in devoting attention to specific components of the game. Those who had training in devoting attention to specific components eventually played the game better than those who simply practiced the entire game without instruction.

Gopher's work empirically demonstrates that Gile's "coordination effort" can be supported as a separate part of the interpreting process. "Attention control is a separate component of a complex skill" (DeGroot, 2000, p. 64). A later work by Gopher points out that attention control can be shifted to tasks other than the one on which the training occurred. "Gopher's work suggests that in training the control of attention may be an advantageous component of a training program in simultaneous interpreting."

Methodological Competence

Methodological competence is the competence that allows the interpreter to know which tools or methods to use in solving the myriad of linguistic problems that arise with every interpreting situation. Roberts (1995) suggests that there are two sub-categories within methodological competence. The first is knowing which mode (consecutive or simultaneous) to use in a specific setting. The other sub-category is the ability to find pertinent lexical data and terminology, or appropriate vocabulary, and use it correctly.

Cultural Competence

• Bicultural competence

Roberts (1995) says that bicultural competence is a "deep knowledge and appreciation of the cultures underlying the working languages, is based on the concept that language is a reflection of culture and that true understanding of a message involves mastery of the language in which it is expressed and an understanding of the culture associated with the language. Bi-cultural competence includes knowledge of the basic beliefs, values, experiences and behaviors characteristic of source language speakers and target language speakers." Appreciation of the differences between source and target language cultures is included in bi-cultural competence. Bi-cultural competence includes sociolinguistic competence.

• Sociolinguistic competence

Gonzalez et al. (1991) emphasize the importance of sociolinguistic competence and say that it is the ability to appropriately use register, or levels of formality or informality, and appropriate speech style for a given setting, such as court or an informal meeting. This competency assumes a deep understanding of both cultures and bi-cultural competence.

Content Competence

Gile calls content competency extralinguistic knowledge (ELK). This refers to the knowledge that the interpreter has about the subject. Sometimes this knowledge is based on the topic alone and is not specifically related to the culture. In other cases, the information is culture specific. In either case, the more familiar the interpreter is with the subject the better. However, it is possible that if the interpreter is too familiar with the subject or is too intimately connected to the subject or the participants, the interpreter's effectiveness will decrease. This could happen if the interpreter's extensive prior knowledge of the topic influences the interpretation. For example, if the topic is auto mechanics and the interpreter is well versed in this topic, there is a temptation for the interpreter to add information that the speaker did not say or to clarify points that were not made clear by the speaker. The interpreter should know something about the topic he or she is interpreting, but should not add facts that the speaker did not include.

The speaker's topic could be related to neither culture, such as auto mechanics, or it could be related to one culture or the other exclusively. An example of a culturally based topic is telecommunication devices for the deaf. Sometimes the topic is not related to the culture of either the source language or the target language. For example, the subject of physics is not related to a specific culture, but may be discussed by members of various cultures.

• Approximation

Neubert (2000) discusses additional aspects of translation competencies that also apply to interpreting. He points out that because you are not necessarily experts in the subjects that you work with, you must acquire the capacity to *approximate* the subject areas to an extent that allows understanding. Neubert suggests that this competence must be open-ended. "Translators are always on the lookout for new ways of saying something. They must always feel the pulse of language" (p.4). The need to be open-ended, or flexible, leads to the need for *creativity* because the source text must be expressed in a different language, with different linguistic and cultural constraints. Creativity in the context of interpretation means that the interpreter uses strongly grounded linguistic skills to render the message effectively, not that the interpreter invents an interpretation that is unrelated to the source text.

Interpersonal Competencies

Interpersonal or non-language-based competencies describe an individual's suitability for working as a professional interpreter. The first is overall suitability for the profession and includes stamina, curiosity, maturity, mental agility, adaptability, tolerance for ambiguity, and tolerance for a wide variety of personalities and situations. Another important personal competency is having a strong command of the non-linguistic intricacies of interpretation. For interpreters who work from signed to spoken languages it is essential to look directly at the signer in either consecutive or simultaneous. The interpreter must be comfortable with eye contact and must not confuse level of eye contact with permission to influence the communicative event more than is inherently necessary. For an in-depth discussion of how the interpreter functions in the context of a dialogic setting, see Metzger (2000). While all of the competencies are important, interpersonal competencies should always be kept in mind. A deficiency in any of the competencies discussed may lead to a skewed interpretation.

In studying simultaneous interpreting, intralingual proficiency, cognitive manipulation, translation, and consecutive interpreting competencies are essential and should be mastered prior to beginning the study of simultaneous interpreting. Sometimes the component skills (linguistic, methodological, and interpersonal) are present, but synthesis of them is lacking. Unless the components are addressed individually and then intentionally synthesized, it is difficult to determine whether a skewed interpretation is caused by lack of mastery of the component skills or the synthesis of the skills. Some of the skills tap more than one essential process. For example, developing automaticity in language processing depends on linguistic skill and cognitive skill.

One way to begin to synthesize the component competencies is to study models of interpretation that allow us to see how competencies fit together into the larger process of interpretation. This introduction addresses some of the competencies that interpreters must have and several models of simultaneous interpreting. Another important feature stressed in this introduction and in the units that follow is that the more practice you have in the subskills of interpreting, the more routinized those skills become. When subskills are strongly routinized, you have more attention to devote to other aspects of the interpreting process that cannot be routinized.

This text provides exercises within a theoretical framework that allows you to build on your existing skills in consecutive interpreting and self-analysis as a way to begin developing simultaneous interpreting skills. Review exercises in consecutive interpreting, followed by "bridging" exercises, allow you to systematically build your simultaneous processing skills in an organized manner. For example, the review exercises allow you to practice rendering the message into the target language in real time without the pressures of simultaneity. If you have used earlier volumes in *The Effective Interpreting Series*, you will be familiar with some of the selections. You may have paraphrased some, translated others, or consecutively interpreted still others. You will work with familiar material in new ways. The familiar material is presented first with pauses to allow for consecutive interpreting and then without pauses to allow for a smooth transition into simultaneous processing of the source message into the target language. In later units you will have the opportunity to work with new material.

UNIT 1

Consecutive Interpreting

This book contains structured practice in the skills that precede and comprise simultaneous interpreting skills and begins with exercises in consecutive interpreting. If you are beyond the beginning stages of an interpreter education program or are already a working interpreter, you can benefit from practicing consecutive interpreting skills, either as a refresher or for professional skill maintenance. Practicing the consecutive interpreting skills in this unit provides you with meaningful and well-organized exercises to review your consecutive interpreting skills.

Practicing interpreters may not have had the benefit of studying the individual skills that make up the interpretation process. Practicing interpreters often search for specific ways to improve their skills. Reviewing well-controlled consecutive interpreting skills can be meaningful and productive practice for the experienced interpreter who wishes to work independently on skill improvement. The spoken English source materials in this unit and other units can be used again in later stages of training.

This unit provides a brief review of the history and uses for consecutive interpreting, a comparison of consecutive and simultaneous interpreting, and a summary of Gile's model of consecutive interpreting. There are six review exercises in this unit. The English source material for these exercises appeared in *The Effective Interpreting Series: Consecutive Interpreting from English*. However, here they appear in a different format and with different questions. This approach allows you to systematically begin the process of bridging from consecutive interpreting to simultaneous interpreting by first reviewing the consecutive process. Since the materials may be familiar, they should serve as excellent warm-up materials and prepare you for the more challenging exercises in the units that follow.

Introduction to Consecutive Interpreting

This introduction provides an overall orientation to consecutive interpreting in signed and spoken languages, its history, uses, relevance to signed language interpreting, and some theoretical information that will help prepare you for the exercises in the unit.

Consecutive interpreting was commonly used prior to the 1940s in the spoken language interpreting community (Gonzalez et al., 1991). After World War II, due to the needs of the court systems in Europe and advances in technology, simultaneous interpreting became more widely used than consecutive interpreting.

Mikkelson (1983, p. 6) says, "Consecutive interpreting is a procedure by which the interpreter listens to a message and concurrently reorganizes the information by means of a highly personalized note-taking system that enables him/her to cast off the external linguistic structure of the message and then transfer its essence to another linguistic structure that is intelligible to his/her audience." Sometimes consecutive interpreters do work without notes when the utterances are short. In consecutive interpreting the interpreter has the option of using note-taking when necessary and appropriate. The exception to this may be when the interpreter is working from ASL to English. Signed language interpreters who use both a signed and a spoken mode will not be able to effectively take notes while watching a signer.

Ilg and Lambert (1996) provide a concise introduction to some of the remarkably accomplished interpreters who used and taught consecutive interpreting. Most interpreters who worked prior to World War II were self-taught and used consecutive interpreting. Some of these interpreters trained other people who later wrote important works that influenced the field.

"Seleskovich was one of the first educators to define the need to teach and practice consecutive interpretation prior to simultaneous interpretation, believing it to be the foundation for all accurate interpretation work" (Russell, 2002, p. 35).

Consecutive Interpreting in Sign Language Interpreting

In the field of sign language interpreting in North America, consecutive interpreting has had an equally important but unacknowledged place in practice and training (Patrie, 1989). Historically, sign language interpreter training programs may not have included consecutive interpreting as a course or skill, simply because its value in training was not realized. Many early educators were familiar with consecutive interpreting since most of the original instructors in interpreter education programs had deaf parents and used consecutive interpreting while interpreting for their parents. Later, in the 1960s, these same people became the first professional interpreters. Still later, in the 1970s, they became the first interpreter educators when interpreter education programs began to spring up nationwide. Legislation to benefit deaf people's access to communication led directly to the establishment of many programs, but the programs, although they reflected the best efforts of the day, often did not meet the growing need for qualified interpreters. The experienced interpreters who suddenly found themselves teaching interpretation often did not have the benefit of curriculum or textbooks and were pioneers in sign language interpreter education.

Since the 1970s consecutive interpreting has become integrated into more curricula. Today the demands on interpreter education programs are higher than ever in terms of accountability. In recent years there has been a slow but steady shift to the realization that time spent on consecutive interpreting in the interpreter education curriculum is crucial to the success of its graduates and is time well spent.

If interpreters are trained to use consecutive interpreting in situations that demand the highest accuracy, then the interpreters will have the confidence and the skill to use consecutive interpreting appropriately. In general, users of signed language interpreting services have come to expect only simultaneous interpreting services. This expectation results from the widespread and nearly exclusive use of simultaneous interpreting. "Despite the significant body of literature from spoken language interpreting which suggests that consecutive interpretation allows for a greater degree of accuracy, the predominant practice of ASL/English interpreters is to provide simultaneous interpreting" (Russell, 2002, p. 41). Often simultaneous interpreting has a detrimentally short processing time. In some settings consecutive interpreting would better serve all participants. Cokely's (1992) findings on simultaneous interpreting in ASL suggest that when interpreters have greater processing time, and therefore larger amounts of the source message, overall errors are reduced. Interpreters must have both skills readily available and must also know which settings would benefit from the use of consecutive rather than simultaneous interpreting.

Frequently Asked Questions

What Are the Differences between Consecutive Interpreting and Simultaneous Interpreting?

Gile (2001, p.3) describes the differences between consecutive interpreting and simultaneous interpreting by making the following five comparisons.

1. In the production effort, the interpreter can devote more attention to the target language output in consecutive interpreting than in simultaneous interpreting.

   Simultaneous interpreting involves processing two languages at once in "working memory." During simultaneous interpreting the interpreter must attend to inhibiting the effect of interference from the source language, while producing the target language output. In consecutive interpreting there is much less likelihood of interference of the source language. The consecutive interpreting process allows the interpreter to take notes and then produce the target language output. In consecutive interpreting the interpreter can devote greater attention to monitoring target language output than is possible during simultaneous interpreting.

2. Target speech occurs under heavier time pressure in simultaneous interpreting than in consecutive interpreting.

   This variable is especially relevant when the source text is very dense or rapid material. In consecutive interpreting, the interpreter can pace himself or herself while the simultaneous interpreter must keep producing target language speech, going at the speaker's pace.

3. During consecutive interpreting the interpreter must decide what to write down and how to write it.

   The processes associated with note-taking are only found in consecutive interpreting, not in simultaneous interpreting.

4. The note-taking process and the slowness of writing during consecutive interpreting create a demand on working memory that does not exist in simultaneous interpreting.

   Learning the specific strategies for note-taking can reduce the cognitive load imposed by the note-taking process during consecutive interpreting.

5. Consecutive interpreting requires more long-term memory involvement than simultaneous interpreting.

Mead (1994) says that simultaneous interpreting is often thought of as the ultimate linguistic skill and that many people are unaware of the existence of consecutive interpreting. However, the "uninitiated" audience is likely to be most impressed by a well-rendered consecutive interpreting performance. Interpreters who have performed both simultaneous interpreting and consecutive interpreting know that the skills involved in each are not easily separable. There may be observable differences between consecutive and simultaneous interpreting but there "is not a clear cut division between skills required for SI [simultaneous interpreting] and those called for in CI [consecutive interpreting]" (p. 26). Because there may be considerable overlap between the two processes, it is wise to keep in mind that the main goal of the consecutive interpreting exercises in this book is to better prepare you for simultaneous interpreting.

What Are the Advantages of Using Consecutive Interpreting?

The main advantage of consecutive interpreting is that it allows for greater accuracy than simultaneous interpreting. Russell (2002) notes that consecutive interpreting allows the interpreter to include information that is crucial to the message but that might be omitted during the pressures of simultaneous interpreting. Examples include vocal intonation, pauses, and repetitions. Russell (2002) reviewed the literature on consecutive interpreting and found that "consecutive interpreting results in much greater accuracy in the transmission of the message" (p. 53).

Another advantage of consecutive interpreting is additional time for reformulation and expression, without ongoing input of the source language. However, this is an advantage that can be lost if the text is long and memory is poor or even average. Additionally, consecutive interpreting is generally more accurate than simultaneous, provided that the interpreter is skilled in using consecutive. Seleskovitch and Lederer (1995) say that consecutive interpreting is more reliable than simultaneous interpreting for extremely technical discussions. This may be true, but only if the interpreter knows how to use consecutive interpreting approaches correctly and has actually practiced using these methods. Even though not all interpreter education programs address the development of consecutive interpreting skills, there is enough anecdotal evidence to suggest that it is a valuable developmental stage in learning simultaneous interpreting.

What Is Note-Taking in Consecutive Interpreting?

Note-taking is one of the main features that distinguishes consecutive interpreting from simultaneous interpreting. Ilg and Lambert's (1997) review of consecutive interpreting shows a wide range of approaches and opinions regarding note-taking in consecutive interpreting. At one end of the continuum are detailed note-taking systems the interpreter uses while listening to the original source message and refers to while rendering the interpretation. At the opposite end of the continuum is the notion held by Seleskovich and others at the Ecole Superieure d'Interprets et de Traducteurs, which suggests that note-taking is not central or beneficial to the process of consecutive interpreting and that recall of the message happens automatically if the message was understood. For spoken language interpreters' note-taking skills play a role in professional consecutive interpretation, but for signed language interpreters, note-taking may only play a role in training. For more information on note-taking in consecutive interpreting see *An Introduction to Basic Note-Taking Skills for Consecutive Interpretation* by Nancy Schweda Nicholson (1993). A special note-taking system for legal situations is described in Fundamentals of Court Interpretation by Gonzalez et al. (1991).

Time Constraints in Consecutive Interpreting

It is tempting to think that the additional time in consecutive interpretation makes the process easier than simultaneous interpretation. This is usually not the case unless the utterances are short. Some interpreters say that consecutive interpreting presents an even greater challenge than simultaneous interpreting due to the increased demands on memory (Bonnichsen and Isbell, 2001). It is difficult to compare the two types of interpreting directly because there are many differences in terms of cognitive demands. Although it may appear at first that consecutive interpretation is more time consuming than simultaneous interpretation, it may be more economical in some instances. Seleskovitch (1978b) points out that consecutive interpreting can actually save time because the "thinking" time afforded to participants during the time the message is rendered into the other language provides time to clarify and distill points of information.

A Model of Consecutive Interpretation

The processes in consecutive interpreting are similar to but not exactly the same as those in simultaneous interpreting. Consecutive interpreting characteristically has pauses in the source message during which the interpretation is rendered. The source message in simultaneous interpreting does not have pauses. Other models for consecutive interpreting may exist, but for clarity's sake only one is presented here.

The components of Gile's Effort Model of consecutive interpretation (2001) follow. Gile explains that the consecutive interpreting Effort Model occurs in two phases. The first phase of the model is listening.

Listening Phase

• Listening effort

This phase includes the effort directed toward comprehension. Comprehension is a non-automatic process for interpreters. Because it is non-automatic, it is subject to capacity restrictions and saturation. For example, if a person is speaking rapidly about a technical topic, then greater demands are placed on the interpreter's listening and analysis effort.

• Production effort (note-taking effort)

In this phase of the model, the interpreter creates a written set of notes. The purpose of taking notes is to help the interpreter remember the message. The interpreter refers to these notes later in the process. Note-taking techniques must be fully developed to provide a consistent advantage for the interpreter in terms of reducing memory load constraints. Interpreters working to and from signed languages will have limited use for note-taking. If the signed language interpreter is working from a spoken to a signed language, it is physically possible that the interpreter could take notes and refer to the notes when rendering the signed interpretation. When working from a signed to a spoken language, it is less likely that the interpreter will be able to take notes due to the physical constraints of simultaneously watching the signed source message and taking notes.

• Short-term memory effort

During the interpreting process working memory, or short-term memory, and long-term memory are necessary and interact continuously. Both of the cognitive operations that deal with short- and long-term memory occur continuously during interpreting and are non-automatic. The information that is processed, even if it is familiar, is probably never exactly the same as a prior exposure to it. For example, when a speaker gives a speech twice on the same topic it will not be exactly the same speech and will be processed using various short- and long-term memory mechanisms.

"In consecutive interpreting the Memory Effort is similar to that used in simultaneous interpreting. However in consecutive, it is associated with the time between the moment information is heard and the moment it is written down or between the moment it is heard and the moment the interpreter decides not to write it down, or between the moment it is heard and the moment it disappears from memory" (p. 179).

Reformulation Phase

In phase two of this model, Gile explains that the interpreter does not have to share processing capacity between varieties of tasks like listening, analysis, and note-taking. "There are no problems arising from an accumulation of tasks under the pressure of time resulting in capacity requirement peaks. The capacity requirements for the first stage of the model are greater than those in the second stage of the model. The second phase of the model includes three efforts" (Gile, 2001, p. 2).

• Note-reading effort

Some processing capacity (PC) is required to read and decipher one's own notes. In order to reduce the PC needed to decipher one's own notes, it is important to practice note-taking and reading one's own notes in advance of the consecutive interpreting event.

Long-term memory effort allows for retrieving information from long-term memory. Interpreters often rely on visual memory, either in the arrangement of their notes to reflect aspects of the source message or by tapping visual memory storage mechanisms to help them sequence the order of events in the speech. This is especially true of signed language interpreters who receive a signed message via visual mechanisms.

• Production effort (producing the message in the target language)

This effort relates to the product of the interpretation. "In simultaneous interpretation, it is defined as the set of operations extending from the mental representation of the message to be delivered to speech planning and the performance of the speech plan. In consecutive interpretation, there are two kinds of production. During the first phase the interpreter listens to the speech and produces notes: during the second phase, he or she produces the target language speech" (Gile, 2001, p. 2).

Gile (2001) describes a major difference between consecutive and simultaneous interpreting. In CI speech comprehension and full production in the target language are separated. The interpreter is then spared short-term memory pressures and the pressures of requirements associated with delivering the message in the target language. The second phase of CI is characterized by greater time and capacity available for speech production. In the first phase, even though the interpreter is driven by the speaker's pace, taking notes is generally easier than rendering the same information simultaneously into spoken language.

Being aware of the aspects and phases of consecutive interpretation can help you focus your available capacities on the tasks that need your immediate attention during the process. Gile explains that when the requirements of the tasks exceed your current capacity, problems are triggered that can lead to failures in interpretation.

For a comprehensive bibliography on consecutive interpreting see Ilg and Lambert (1996).

Study Questions

1. In which settings could consecutive interpreting be used?

____

____

____

____

____

____

2. What is the value of studying a model of interpretation?

____

____

____

____

____

3. List the components of Gile's 2001 model of consecutive interpretation. Be sure you understand and can explain all components.

____

____

____

____

____

4. What are the advantages of using consecutive interpreting?

____

____

____

____

____

____

____

The exercises in Units 1 and 2 provide a unique method for transitioning from consecutive to simultaneous interpreting by using warm or familiar material. In Unit 1 you render the interpretation during the pauses and can stop the tape if you need to. In Unit 2 there are short pauses in the tape to help you bridge from consecutive to simultaneous interpreting. This approach allows you to shift from consecutive processing to simultaneous processing gradually. This is a structured method that allows you to focus on the addition of simultaneity in interpreting process without the pressure associated with comprehension, transfer, and reformulation that occurs when using cold source material.

EXERCISES IN CONSECUTIVE INTERPRETING

There are six exercises in this unit. These selections appeared in *The Effective Interpreting Series: Consecutive Interpreting from English.* These six exercises provide an opportunity to review and practice consecutive interpreting before going on to simultaneous. You will not need to take notes for any of the exercises in this unit. These six selections will appear again in Unit 2 of this book, but with shorter pauses. Each selection has three study questions. There is no follow-up for this unit.

EXERCISE 1.1

My Big Move

LORRAINE OLDHAM

Directions

This selection is approximately 2 minutes long. Find a quiet place to work where you will not be interrupted. Answer study question 1. Find the video selection. Adjust the volume as necessary and be sure you can see the TV monitor clearly. Begin by allowing yourself time to focus on the speaker's face. When you hear the beep tone, pause the video to give yourself time to render the interpretation. Record your consecutive interpretation and then answer the remaining study questions.

Study Questions

1. Describe the context and participants for this interpretation based on the title of the exercise and the picture of the speaker.

____

____

____

2. Did you react to the message? Were your reactions observable? Did you react to your interpretation? If yes, was your reaction to your interpretation observable?

____

____

____

____

3. How stressful was it to interpret this passage? If it was the first time you interpreted this passage circle the answer that most closely describes your reaction and explain why. If this was the second time you interpreted this passage how did the stress level compare to the first time you interpreted it? Circle your selection. Did your interpretation show your level of stress?

First time:

Not stressful   Moderately stressful   Stressful   Very stressful

Second time:

Less stressful   Slightly less stressful   Slightly more stressful   More stressful

Transcript for *My Big Move,* Lorraine Oldham

Hi. I'm Lorraine Oldham and I'd like to tell you about a recent experience that I've had that I have learned an awful lot from. // Umm, I was recently divorced and—almost after 30 years of marriage—and it came as a shock to me when everything fell apart. // I had to move from the east coast to the west coast once again. // My daughter and I made a decision that it would be best for us to return to our family and friends that we had for so long in San Diego, California. //

Uh, the decision was a long and hard one, but when I finally got into the program and decided that I was going to do it, the momentum just carried me through. // My daughter went ahead of me and I took a month after she left to make all the preparations for the move. // And the scary part for me was the fact that I realized that I had to drive cross-country, 3,200 miles between Boston and San Diego totally by myself. // And I postponed it as long as I could because I was very frightened. // And once I got into the car and started my journey, I realized that it was the best decision that I could have ever made. // As frightening as it was, I realized that this experience was going to take me through life and I was very glad that I did it. // And now I'm here in San Diego and I am successful and I am going forward and my life finally has meaning again. Thank you. //

EXERCISE 1.2

Preparing Chicken Fajitas

ELLA PERKIN

Directions

This selection is approximately 4 minutes long. Find a quiet place to work where you will not be interrupted. Answer study question 1. Find the video selection. Adjust the volume as necessary and be sure you can see the TV monitor clearly. Begin by allowing yourself time to focus on the speaker's face. When you hear the beep tone, pause the video to give yourself time to render the interpretation. Record your consecutive interpretation and then answer the remaining study questions.

Study Questions

1. Describe the context and participants for this interpretation based on the title of the exercise and the picture of the speaker.

   ____

   ____

2. Write one sentence that states the main idea of the selection.

   ____

   ____

3. What would happen if you committed to any one of the details you envisioned in your interpretation and later found that they were incorrect?

   ____

   ____

   ____

   ____

   ____

Transcript for *Preparing Chicken Fajitas,* Ella Perkin

Hi. My name is Ella Perkin and I'm going to give you directions on how to make chicken fajitas. // I'm one of those people who likes to cook things in the microwave, and if you're one of those people who don't know how to cook, this is a very easy thing to make. //

First you need to go to the grocery store and buy some boneless, skinless chicken, // some tort—flour tortillas, salsa, one green pepper, one red pepper and an onion. // Then you take the chicken and cut it on a cutting board into small pieces. // And cook it in a big wok pan. // You should cook it and make sure it's thoroughly cooked because if it's a little raw in the middle you could get very sick. //

When the chicken is thoroughly cooked you take it out of the pan and put it onto a plate. // And now you want to cut the vegetables. But before you cut the vegetables you want to make sure that you wash off the cutting board and the knife so that, again, you don't get sick from the raw chicken that was just on there. //

You cut the green pepper and you want to make sure that you take the core out of the green pepper and cut it into small pieces. // And cut the onion into small pieces. And when you cut the onion you might start crying. // Then you cut the red pepper and it's just like the green pepper—you cut the core out and then you slice it into pieces and then cut it the opposite way into small squares. //

Now you need to add some oil into the pan before you cook the vegetables because the vegetables don't have any fat in them like the chicken does, so if you don't put oil into the pan they will stick to the bottom of the pan. // Then you—now you put the vegetables into the pan and cook them for a few minutes 'til they are slightly crisp and brown. // Now you can add the chicken back into the pan. And also I forgot to mention earlier that you also need to buy a packet of chicken fajita spice mix at the grocery store. // You add that into the pan with the chicken and the vegetables and one cup of water. //

And you put this now onto a lower heat and mix it for a few minutes and the water will thicken up into a nice thick sauce. // You will now take the tortillas and just pop them in the microwave for a minute. // And now take the fajita mixture, put it into a bowl and you can just have a little nice buffet and this should serve five to six people, and it makes a nice dinner. //

EXERCISE 1.3

Big Grandma

DAVID BURNIGHT

Directions

This selection is approximately 4 1/2 minutes long. Find a quiet place to work where you will not be interrupted. Answer study question 1. Find the video selection. Adjust the volume as necessary and be sure you can see the TV monitor clearly. Begin by allowing yourself time to focus on the speaker's face. When you hear the beep tone, pause the video to give yourself time to render the interpretation. Record your consecutive interpretation and then answer the remaining study questions.

Study Questions

1. Describe the context and participants for this interpretation based on the title of the exercise and the picture of the speaker.

2. Did you remember the information based on prior experiences with a grandparent or older woman you know? How did your memory of your previous interpretation of this material affect your current interpretation?

3. How stressful was it to interpret this passage? If it was the first time you interpreted this passage, circle the answer that most closely describes your reaction and explain why. If this was the second time you interpreted this passage, how did the stress level compare to the first time you interpreted it? Circle your selection. Did your interpretation show your level of stress?

   First time:

   Not stressful   Moderately stressful   Stressful   Very stressful

   Second time:

   Less stressful   Slightly less stressful   Slightly more stressful   More stressful

Transcript for *Big Grandma,* David Burnight

Hi, my name is David Burnight. I would like to tell you a little bit about my "Big Grandma." // Some of my favorite memories are about Big Grandma. I call her Big Grandma because I also had a little grandma. // Big Grandma wasn't fat, she was just big. // She grew up in Illinois of pioneer settler stock, and she just had big bones, and was a big woman. // When my mother was 13 Grandpa died, and so Grandma took over and went to work and raised all three children herself. //

When I came along Grandma was living about half the time with our family and half the time with her son, so I always considered her a member of our family. // She would wash dishes and do the ironing, and help my mother a lot, and I enjoyed Big Grandma. //

We had a cabin up in the mountains and would go up every June and Grandma would go with us; // and after the sweeping and dusting and bringing down the cobwebs was done, Grandma would go for hikes with me. // She was an old lady, but she was a sturdy old lady. // She always took along a big walking stick, and she told me that it was to kill rattlesnakes with. // She had grown up in a place where the horses grazing on the prairie in Illinois were sometimes bitten by rattlesnakes, which would lie in the prairie clover. // And so Grandma hated rattlesnakes and whenever she would see one she would kill it. // And as a matter of fact, when we'd find one on our hikes on the trail, Grandma would beat its head off with her walking stick. //

I think one of the funniest things that happened was one day when my dog Laddie cornered a skunk underneath our cabin. // Wow, what a smell that was! // But Grandma was not even concerned. // That was the day we discovered that Grandma had lost her sense of smell. // And, as a matter of fact now we understood why she'd been complaining lately that food just didn't taste as good as it used to, because when your sense of smell goes you lose your sense of taste, too. //

Grandma had been born in 1860 and she told me that when she was five years old her father took her down to the railway crossing to see President Lincoln's funeral train go by. // To have that kind of living contact with our nation's history always thrilled me when I thought about it. // Grandma lived to be almost 102, and on her 100th birthday President Eisenhower sent her a birthday card. // Of course, he sent birthday cards to every 100-year-old person, but we always thought that it was very special because Grandma was very special to us. //

EXERCISE 1.4

Fusion Cooking

ARLENE FONG CRAIG

Directions

This selection is approximately 6 minutes long. Find a quiet place to work where you will not be interrupted. Answer study question 1. Find the video selection. Adjust the volume as necessary and be sure you can see the TV monitor clearly. Begin by allowing yourself time to focus on the speaker's face. When you hear the beep tone, pause the video to give yourself time to render the interpretation. Record your consecutive interpretation and then answer the remaining study questions.

Study Questions

1. Describe the context and participants for this interpretation based on the title of the exercise and the picture of the speaker.

2. Examine your interpretation to determine whether your reaction to your interpretation was observable. If you find that you reacted to your interpretation, explain why.

3. Did you become fatigued while interpreting? Did fatigue cause any errors in your interpretation? If yes, explain.

Transcript for *Fusion Cooking,* Arlene Fong Craig

Hello. I'm Arlene Fong Craig. There's been a lot of talk lately about "fusion cooking." // But in my opinion, fusion cooking has been happening ever since immigration started. // Any time a people or a culture moves across boundaries, they take other aspects of their culture with them. They keep some things, they discard others, and they transform still others, other items. //

So this is my recipe for fusion Chinese-American roast turkey. You need a 22- to 25-pound turkey, eviscerated, cleaned, and patted dry. // You'll need, for the marinade, five parts low-sodium soy sauce, four parts of liquor, preferably a good bourbon or Scotch, because the smoky, peaty flavor really blends well with the other flavors of the turkey // and the ingredients, you'll need three parts of mashed or minced garlic and ginger, two parts honey, and one part Asian sesame oil maybe one or two glogs of that. // Combine all of those ingredients and be sure that you thoroughly coat the turkey, both inside and out. //

You'll need to put the turkey in a roasting pan or some other container that is nonreactive, perhaps stainless steel, glass, or a ceramic such as Corningware. // You'll need to marinate the turkey in the refrigerator for at least 24 hours on each side, or if you cannot do that, a half a day on each side. //

When you're ready to roast the turkey, take it out of the refrigerator about an hour beforehand. // Pre-heat the oven about 30 minutes before you're ready to start, to 500°. You'll need a very hot oven in order to sear the bird and to seal in the juices. //

When you're ready to start roasting, place the turkey breast-side down in a non-stick roasting rack, they make Teflon roasting racks, will serve the best, and cover the turkey with an aluminum foil tent. // You can crimp the edges and just loosely cover the back of the bird. And be sure to cover the wing tips and the drumstick ends, also with aluminum foil. //

Roast the turkey, undisturbed, for about 20 minutes—I guarantee it won't burn—and then after 20 minutes, reduce the temperature to 350°. // You'll need to baste the turkey every 15–20 minutes regularly during the cooking time. //

After about two hours for a 25-pound turkey—Oh, I beg your pardon, I forgot: You need, after about an hour, you can remove the aluminum foil tent, and perhaps, the protection from the wing tips and the drumsticks. // Continue basting, and after about two hours, take the turkey out of the oven and flip it over to the breast side. // And the method I've found most useful, after a lot of burned fingers and burned hands, is to take two old but very clean wash cloths, wrap them around your hands, and just insert your hands into the cavities of the bird and flip it over. // And that's really the best and the safest way to turn the turkey over in a whole piece. Be sure to baste it before you put it back into the oven, and to put the tent over the breast, and to protect the wing tips again. //

Continue basting, and after about two hours, give it a test. This is four hours total cooking time. // And if the juices run clear from the thigh, and if, when you press the meat, it does not spring back, then you know the turkey is done. If you like your turkey better more well done, you can leave it in a little longer, but continue to baste the bird. //

As my husband would say, I like my poultry "just done." And he'll say, "Here bird, jump up on the table!" And that's when I know it's ready! //

Be sure you let the turkey rest for 30 minutes for a bird this size before you start carving. In this way, the juices will shrink back into the bird, and the meat will keep its integrity when you begin carving. // So, there you have it: Fusion Chinese-American roast turkey! //

EXERCISE 1.5

My Hobby

JANET PERKIN

Directions

This selection is approximately 6 1/4 minutes long. Find a quiet place to work where you will not be interrupted. Answer study question 1. Find the video selection. Adjust the volume as necessary and be sure you can see the TV monitor clearly. Begin by allowing yourself time to focus on the speaker's face. When you hear the beep tone, pause the video to give yourself time to render the interpretation. Record your consecutive interpretation and then answer the remaining study questions.

Study Questions

1. Describe the context and participants for this interpretation based on the title of the exercise and the picture of the speaker.

2. Review your interpretation and rate its intelligibility by circling the choice that most closely describes your intelligibility on the scale provided below.

   Completely intelligible   Mostly intelligible   Not intelligible

   Briefly explain your choice.

3. Circle the selection that best describes your volume.

   Loud enough voice/large enough signs

   Average loudness/visibility

   Too soft/ small signs

   Briefly explain your choice.

Transcript for *My Hobby*, by Janet Perkin

Hi. My name is Janet Perkin and I'm going to tell you about my hobby, which is antique collecting. // I think this first started when I visited my grandparents' house, which was a 17th century farmhouse on, um, the outskirts of Sheffield. // And we used to visit there every Sunday, and I'm going to tell you what the inside of the house was like compared with what we live in today. // First of all, the kitchen itself had no electricity. // They had to cook on a black, leaded stove, uh, with the heat of coal from the fire. // This was kep—kept gleaming all the time by my grandmother, who polished it regularly. // There was a huge pine table in the kitchen with an old red settle where the farm workers used to come and sit and have their breakfast and lunch. // Also, there was an old stone sink there—we had no running water. They had to go into the garden and draw water from the well. // At nighttime we all had to use a paraffin lamp to heat—to light the room and then a candle we used to take to the bedroom. // In the bedroom we had beautiful pottery jug and water—a water jug to wash with, instead of having the bathroom. //

Later on when my grandparents died I attended the auction. Uh, where, unfortunately, everything was auctioned to the general public and so many of the things were lost to the family. // There's many things I wish I would've been able to have, like the old monk's bench, which was in fact a—a bench which also made into a table. A very rare piece of furniture. // I did manage to collect an old green platter and a gold Noritake coffee set, which I still have today. //

Later on in life I did inherit other pieces from members of the family, such as a grandfather clock from my mother-in-law which had been in the family many, many years. And we still have it today. //

When I was in my late twenties I got the real antique bug and I used to attend many estate sales, auctions, even garage sales. // And throughout the years I've collected a wonderful collection of Victorian, uh, furniture. In fact if you were to enter my living room today you would see a beautiful mahogany sideboard, and on that you would see a beautiful Victorian silver, uh, tea set, coffee pot. And then also in the room you would see a beautiful chaise lounge—for reclining on. // And it's a beautiful room with lots of prints, botanical prints that were popular in Victorian times. //

Now, my family room, which is very, very different, reminds a lot of people of a British pub. // Because you'll see a big fireplace, red brick, with a big oak beam across. Now, on the fireplace there are many, many horse brasses, uh, which are brass lu—uh, good luck charms used on the old farm horses years and years ago. // These adorn the mantelpiece with many brass candlesticks, miner's lamps from the old coal mines and also brass rail lamps. // Now, also in the family room you will find a huge oak table very similar to the one in my grandmother's kitchen. Here is where our family meets every Sunday evening. // We try and keep the same tradition that we had in my grandmother's time of meeting on Sunday evening and having a family meal together. // In fact you'll also find a beautiful Welsh dresser there with many, many pieces of blue and white china. //

Now today, my children just don't appreciate many of my antiques, but I hope that one day they will, because, uh, these are things that have been treasured through members of the family and through my life, and I hope one day they'll come to love antiques just as I do. //

EXERCISE 1.6

Sailing

CHRIS LEWNES

Directions

This selection is approximately 6 1/2 minutes long. Find a quiet place to work where you will not be interrupted. Answer study question 1. Find the video selection. Adjust the volume as necessary and be sure you can see the TV monitor clearly. Begin by allowing yourself time to focus on the speaker's face. Record your consecutive interpretation and then answer study questions 2–5.

Study Questions

1. Describe the context and participants for this interpretation based on the title of the exercise and the picture of the speaker.

2. What strategies did you use to focus your listening on the speaker's message? Write a single sentence that describes how you focused your listening.

3. What happened to your listening process when you encountered jargon or new vocabulary?

4. Review your interpretation. Refer to the transcript of this passage and compare it to your interpretation. Rate your listening and analysis efforts during this interpretation.

   Listening dropped off with fatigue   Maintained accurate listening

5. Refer to your answer to question 4. If you selected "Listening dropped off with fatigue," locate two errors in the interpretation that correspond to where you felt fatigue. Circle the corresponding section of the transcript.

   All interpreters experience fatigue at some point in the interpreting process. Becoming more aware of how fatigue affects listening and, later, the interpretation is important.

Transcript for *Sailing,* Chris Lewnes

Hello. My name is Chris Lewnes. // Today I'd like to talk about my favorite hobby. That's sailing. // Sailing to me is more than just trying to get from one place to another. // I'd like to describe the basic configuration of generally the small boats that I like to sail. //

They're configured as a sloop, which is one mast; // a ketch, two masts; a yawl, also two masts, // however the aft mast is behind the steering wheel; // and a schooner—a schooner has two masts but the aft mast is larger than the forward mast. //

My boat is configured as a sloop // a single mast with a foresail and a mainsail. // In sailing, it's not always point-to-point to get from one place to another. // One has to be aware of the wind, and the direction from which the wind is coming. // In order to get your boat to sail the way you want it to sail you have to be aware of the wind, // and aware of how to trim the sails to get the benefit from the wind to move your boat. //

The best point of sail for a sailboat is with the wind on the beam—90 degrees to the sail. // One can sail all day beautifully that way. // The most difficult way to sail is to get to a point that is upwind; // in other words, if there's an island you'd like to go to here off San Diego // I like to go to Catalina. // Generally speaking, because of the prevailing wind, // Catalina is directly into the wind from where I want to go. // I can't sail directly there. // So I have to do what's called "tacking." // I've got to sail my boat as efficiently as I can upwind, // which is about 35 degrees to the wind. // I can only get within 35 degrees of the prevailing wind. // So I'll sail as close as I can to 35 degrees // on a course for as long as I think necessary, // and then I'll have to turn to put the boat on the other "tack" as we call it, // with the wind 35 degrees on the other side of the boat. // Therefore the course would look like a zigzag back and forth to my destination. //

Now, depending upon my skill and the layout of the boat // I can perhaps get there quicker than somebody else. // Of course, if somebody else has a better boat and his skills are better, he's gonna beat me there. // That's part of the challenge and the fun of sailing. // Now, we call that sailing uphill. // Of course, just like everything else if you go uphill there's gonna be a reward coming downhill. // Coming back from Catalina, if the wind is the same then it's a beautiful "run" back to San Diego. // A run is with the wind at our back. // So I'll put the sails all the way out, gather as much wind as I can and float effersly—effortlessly back to San Diego. // That's the ideal condition. //

Of course, having skills and being experienced and knowing how to sail enables one to sail in virtually all types of weather, // knowing that, uh, how much your boat can handle; how much wind you can handle; // where to put the sails; how much sail to expose, // how much sail to take in during heavy weather; // are all things that one should know to make sailing pleasurable, safe, and a long-time enjoyable hobby. //

Progress Tracking Sheet

Use this sheet to track your progress with the exercises you have completed. After performing the exercise (one or two times), answering the study questions, and doing the follow-up, fill in the tracking sheet. Note the date that you completed the exercise and give an indication of your level of accomplishment. You can use either a quantitative or a qualitative approach to track your progress.

Exercise Number	Date	First Performance	Study Questions	Follow-up Activity	Questions and Reminders	Date	Second Performance
Exercise 1.1 Quantitative							
Qualitative							
Exercise 1.2 Quantitative							
Qualitative							
Exercise 1.3 Quantitative							
Qualitative							
Quantitative Totals							

Exercise Number	Date	First Performance	Study Questions	Follow-up Activity	Questions and Reminders	Date	Second Performance
Exercise 1.4 Quantitative							
Qualitative							
Exercise 1.5 Quantitative							
Qualitative							
Exercise 1.6 Quantitative							
Qualitative							
Quantitative Totals							

UNIT 2 Bridging to Simultaneous Interpreting

This unit provides specific practice in transitioning from consecutive to simultaneous interpreting. The shift from consecutive to simultaneous interpreting is difficult. To ease this transition and build confidence, specific exercises have been developed. It is important to allow yourself time to experience the shift from consecutive to simultaneous with low stress, no-risk exercises. Adding simultaneity to the interpreting process is a specific aspect of your training and should be practiced as such. The exercises allow you to work with material with which you are already familiar. These are the exercise you consecutively interpreted in Unit 1. In Unit 1 you were encouraged to stop the source tape when you heard the beep tone. In this unit the exercises have pauses that will provide you with additional time, but you should not pause the source tape. You should continue interpreting, even if you have to omit some details. If you find these exercises challenging, repeat them until you are comfortable with the process and your interpretations are accurate. The transcripts that accompany each selection have marks to indicate where the pauses are located.

In addition to developing simultaneity, you will also have the opportunity to consider four additional factors in your interpretation: your perceived level of stress, processing time, self-monitoring, and self-correction. Self-monitoring and self-correction will be addressed again in later units.

Stress Levels

Simultaneous interpreting is a highly demanding process. Most interpreters realize that some factors in the interpreting process cannot be controlled, such as the speaker's rate of delivery, the content of the talk, the audience reaction to the speaker, and background noise. However, it is important to realize that there are some variables under your control. Situations that can be described as stressful by some people are experienced as merely challenging by others. Sometimes the difference can be attributed to one's perception and attitude, but a positive attitude alone is not enough to overcome stress.

Because many interpreters experience stress while interpreting, it is important to examine the issue of stress in this context. According to Zeier (1997), "Stress is a commonly used term for a wide area of problems associated with physiological, psychological and social human activities" (p.231). Zeier explains that there is no generally accepted scientific definition for stress but that it has two main components: "the experience of a threatening and strenuous situation and the uncertainty whether one is able to cope with the situation." According to Zeier those who experience stress in the workplace are likely to be those who "cannot control workload or foresee critical situations such as air traffic controllers, doctors and nurses in emergency rooms or intensive care units or simultaneous interpreters" (p. 232). It is validating to see that the stress associated with simultaneous interpreting is as high as that in other critically important professions.

Simultaneous interpreting involves a host of complex cognitive processes that are tapped successively and simultaneously. One reason why the task of simultaneous interpretation is stressful is the amount of information that is processed by the interpreter per unit of time. "During a regular 30-minute turn, working from an original speaker whose speaking speed is between 100 and 130 words per minute, considered more or less comfortable depending on the source language involved, an interpreter processes and delivers final copy of an average of 3000 to 3900 words, being equivalent to approximately 12 to 15 type written double spaced pages. With fast speakers a speaking rate of 135 to 189 words per minute, the interpreter's output can increase to 4050-5400 words or 16 to 22 pages per 30-minute turn. As a comparison the output of translators working in an international organization varies between 3 and 10 pages per day" (Moser-Mercer et al., 1998, p. 243 in Zeier, 1997). Knowing that interpreters process between 100 and 189 words per minute helps us to understand that the process is highly demanding even for the most well-trained and experienced interpreters.

Zeier (1997) says that stress really has three main aspects. One is the stimuli that produce the stress reaction, such as how fast the speaker is speaking. Another is the physical and behavioral reaction to the stimuli. For example, if the interpreter has never interpreted for a rapid speaker, that interpreter's physical and behavioral reactions will contribute to perceived levels of stress. The third is other intervening variables. The intervening variables are those that account for whether an event is perceived as stressful by an individual. The experience of stress is generally subjective.

When an event is perceived as stressful, coping behaviors come into play. Zeier says that there are two types of coping behavior, active and passive. Active response to stress is usually described as the "fight or flight" response. When a person senses that they are losing or about to lose control of events in their immediate surroundings, they are likely to want to use some form of active coping behavior. When an individual does not know which coping behavior to select, passive coping mechanisms take over. Passive coping responses include "avoidance, resignation, feelings of inferiority, and lack of self-confidence to severe depression" (Zeier, 1997, p. 233).

Perception allows us to notice events and objects in our environment. Sometimes we find that difficult or challenging situations can evoke fear. When we perceive a situation as challenging, threatening, or fear producing, our energy resources tend to be focused on dealing with the threat or fear, in this case, of failing to correctly interpret. This actually takes the interpreter's attention away from interpreting and focuses all available systems on coping with fear. Alternatively, when we see that our interpretation product is not really directly tied to our well-being or safety, we can more accurately perceive ourselves in relation to our work. In reminding ourselves that we have a choice regarding how we respond to stress, we can improve our control over the interpretation process. Even though interpreting is difficult, challenging, and nerve wracking at times, it is still possible to remind ourselves that even in difficult situations we can maintain composure and a positive outlook and attitude.

An attitude that includes a realistic view of your skills as they relate to the demands of the setting allows you to be alert but not fearful. When you can remain alert but relaxed you can better manage the linguistic and interpersonal challenges within the interpretation process. Using your energy to maintain high levels of stress takes away from available energy resources that you could use for managing the interpretation process. Choosing to maintain a positive attitude during the interpretation process can positively affect the interpretation and the other people involved in the interpreted event.

In this unit you will be asked to notice your level of stress in reaction to the exercise. Stress levels can be felt internally and can cause you to feel anxious or unsure about your choices. Sometimes these internal states cause interpreters to think negative thoughts about the interpretations. If you are thinking negative thoughts about your performance or creating verbal or nonverbal commentary about your work, you are automatically adding stress and taking up valuable cognitive energy.

Processing Time

Processing time is the time you use to perceive the source message, mentally develop an interpretation, and deliver it. Various authors have written about the importance of processing time in interpretation. It is also called decalage or lag time. Most authors agree that, "interpreters with greater control of decalage skills tend to make fewer errors" (Lambert, 1988, p. 49).

Ingram (1984) says that processing time refers to the span of time between the interpreter's perception of the source language and the subsequent production of the target language rendition. It is the period of time between the interpreter's input and output. Cokely (1986) studied four interpreters to analyze the effect of processing time on number of errors or miscues during the interpretation. He found that interpreters who could use the longest amount of processing time tended to make fewer errors. Cokely noted that interpreters who used a two-second processing time made four times as many errors as those who used a four-second processing time. Those who used a four-second processing time made twice as many errors as those who used a six-second processing time. Cokely summarizes the results of his study by saying, "The greater lag time, the more information available; the more information available, the greater the level of comprehension" (1986, p. 67).

The importance of being able to use processing time well in the interpretation process cannot be overstated. When working on the exercises in this unit, notice your processing time. Since you already know the content of the source text and have already interpreted it, you can confidently allow yourself to listen to an idea unit before rendering the corresponding interpretation. If you become anxious, you are likely to use a shorter processing time and start to rush your interpretation. When you shorten your processing time you are more likely to have errors in your interpretation.

Self-Monitoring

Self-monitoring allows you to compare the source message with the interpreted message in the target language. This comparison process requires that you have sufficient memory to allow you to accurately remember what you heard or saw in the source language, how you interpreted it, and sufficient command of both languages to determine whether the source and target languages are equivalent. It might seem that self-monitoring only means listening to your interpretation, but in reality, the interpretation must be compared to the source message. As you develop your simultaneous interpreting skills you must constantly be making comparisons between the source and target messages in order to monitor your accuracy.

As you work on the exercises in this unit, notice how you monitor your interpreting in an ongoing fashion. This may be a new skill for you if this is your first attempt at simultaneous interpreting. Simultaneous interpreting requires that you monitor your output while continuously processing new input. This continuous self-monitoring is one of the main differences between consecutive and simultaneous interpreting. Later in this book you will have additional practice in self-monitoring and self-correction.

Self-Correction

Self-correction naturally follows the self-monitoring process. Sometimes this process is called repair. If you have accurately monitored your output you can detect errors and correct them. Self-correction may be a new skill for you if this is the first time you have attempted simultaneous interpreting. It is important to allow yourself some time to develop the skill of monitoring your interpretation, noticing errors, and correcting them. At first you may find that simply monitoring your interpretation takes up most of your cognitive energy. With time and practice you can expand your range to include noticing and correcting errors.

In this unit and in those that follow you will have the opportunity to notice and correct errors in real time. To make a correction in your interpretation, simply render the corrected version as soon as you have formulated it and continue interpreting. This correction process could cause you to momentarily lose your place in your interpretation. If this happens, simply pick up the process as quickly as you can. As the result of losing your place, you may have an omission in your interpretation. This can be seen as a normal developmental stage and should not be seen as a serious error. When you are concentrating on learning a new skill, an already established skill may suffer temporary setbacks. As you become more familiar with learning how to correct your work in real time, there will be fewer omissions.

Sometimes interpreters point out to the target audience that the interpreter has made an error. This may be feasible in some circumstances but takes additional time and is not recommended if simultaneous is a new skill. For example, if you choose to add the words "interpreter error" to the corrected interpretation, it takes additional time to say these extra words. Sometimes this addition can further confuse the target language audience. Over time and with practice you will be able to determine whether it is appropriate to point out that there is an error in the interpretation or to simply correct it and go on with the interpretation. Remember that self-correction does not include self-criticism. All interpreters make errors at some time or another. A later unit in this book focuses on this topic in more depth.

In this unit you will practice with selections that you consecutively interpreted in Unit 1. These selections do not have any pauses. If you feel stress while you are interpreting these selections, do your best to regain your composure and keep going, even if you have to omit some details. Remember that this unit is designed to help you develop the feel for simultaneous processing in real time. If you find that you need more practice in this area you can use the selections in *The Effective Interpreting Series: Consecutive Interpreting from English*, but do not stop the tape. Even though those selections have pauses and beeps you should allow the tape to run continuously if you are using it to bridge to simultaneous interpreting.

EXERCISES IN BRIDGING TO SIMULTANEOUS

These selections are the same ones you consecutively interpreted in Unit 1. In this unit the source selections have slight pauses (but no beeps). The additional time provided by the pauses will reduce the stress associated with the shift into simultaneous interpreting. You should interpret each selection without stopping. If you need to omit some detail in order to keep going, then do so. The goal in interpreting is to be as accurate as possible and include as much detail as possible, but for the beginning stages of the process it is acceptable to omit some detail in order to learn the feel of the simultaneous process. There is no five-step follow-up in this unit.

EXERCISE 2.1

My Big Move

LORRAINE OLDHAM

Directions

This selection is approximately 2 minutes long. Find a quiet place to work where you will not be interrupted. Describe the context and participants for this interpretation. Adjust the volume as necessary and be sure you can see the TV monitor clearly. Begin by allowing yourself time to focus on the speaker's face. Record your consecutive interpretation and then answer the study questions. The passage has brief pauses in it at the places where you rendered the consecutive interpretation but no beep tones. These pauses allow you additional processing time. Do not pause the source tape. If you miss a few words or ideas, resume interpreting again as soon as you can.

Study Questions

1. Describe the context and participants for this interpretation.

___

___

2. Rate your level of stress during simultaneous interpretation of this passage. Briefly explain your rating.

1	2	3	4	5
No stress	Some	Moderate	High	Very high

___

___

3. Rate your management of processing time. Briefly explain your rating.

1	2	3	4	5
No stress	Some	Moderate	High	Very high

4. Rate your self-monitoring. Briefly explain your rating.

1	2	3	4	5
Excellent	Good	Fair	Poor	Nonexistent

5. Rate yourself on resuming the interpretation if you faltered. Briefly explain your rating.

1	2	3	4	5
Excellent	Good	Fair	Poor	Nonexistent

6. Rate your product for accuracy. Briefly explain your rating.

1	2	3	4	5
Excellent	Good	Fair	Poor	Nonexistent

Transcript for *My Big Move*, by Lorraine Oldham

Hi. I'm Lorraine Oldham and I'd like to tell you about a recent experience that I've had that I have learned an awful lot from. // Umm, I was recently divorced and—almost after 30 years of marriage—and it came as a shock to me when everything fell apart. // I had to move from the east coast to the west coast once again. // My daughter and I made a decision that it would be best for us to return to our family and friends that we had for *so* long in San Diego, California. //

Uh, the decision was a long and hard one, but when I finally got into the program and decided that I was going to do it, the momentum just carried me through. // My daughter went ahead of me and I took a month after she left to make all the preparations for the move. // And the scary part for me was the fact that I realized that I had to drive cross-country, 3,200 miles between Boston and San Diego totally by myself. // And I postponed it as long as I could because I was very frightened. // And once I got into the car and started my journey, I realized that it was the best decision that I could have ever made. // As frightening as it was, I realized that this experience was going to take me through life and I was very glad that I did it. // And now I'm here in San Diego and I am successful and I am going forward and my life finally has meaning again. Thank you. //

EXERCISE 2.2

Preparing Chicken Fajitas

ELLA PERKIN

Directions

This selection is approximately 4 minutes long. Find a quiet place to work where you will not be interrupted. Answer study question 1. Find the video selection. Adjust the volume as necessary and be sure you can see the TV monitor clearly. Begin by allowing yourself time to focus on the speaker's face. Record your consecutive interpretation and then answer the study questions. The passage has brief pauses in it at the places where you rendered the consecutive interpretation but no beep tones. These pauses allow you additional processing time. Do not pause the source tape. If you miss a few words or ideas, resume interpreting again as soon as you can.

Study Questions

1. Describe the context and participants for this interpretation based on the title of the exercise and the picture of the speaker.

 ____

 ____

 ____

2. Rate your level of stress during simultaneous interpretation of this passage. Briefly explain your rating.

1	2	3	4	5
No stress	Some	Moderate	High	Very high

 ____

 ____

3. Rate your management of processing time. Briefly explain your rating.

1	2	3	4	5
Excellent	Good	Fair	Poor	Nonexistent

 ____

 ____

4. Rate your self-monitoring. Briefly explain your rating.

1	2	3	4	5
Excellent	Good	Fair	Poor	Nonexistent

 ____

 ____

5. Rate yourself on resuming the interpretation if you faltered. Briefly explain your rating.

1	2	3	4	5
Excellent	Good	Fair	Poor	Nonexistent

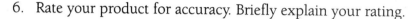

6. Rate your product for accuracy. Briefly explain your rating.

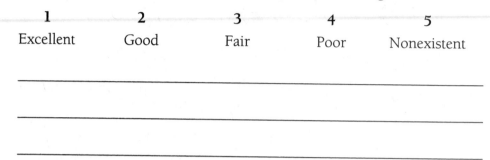

1	2	3	4	5
Excellent	Good	Fair	Poor	Nonexistent

Transcript for *Preparing Chicken Fajitas,* Ella Perkin

Hi. My name is Ella Perkin and I'm going to give you directions on how to make chicken fajitas. // I'm one of those people who likes to cook things in the microwave, and if you're one of those people who don't know how to cook, this is a very easy thing to make. //

First you need to go to the grocery store and buy some boneless, skinless chicken, // some tort—flour tortillas, salsa, one green pepper, one red pepper and an onion. // Then you take the chicken and cut it on a cutting board into small pieces. // And cook it in a big wok pan. // You should cook it and make sure it's thoroughly cooked because if it's a little raw in the middle you could get very sick. //

When the chicken is thoroughly cooked you take it out of the pan and put it onto a plate. // And now you want to cut the vegetables. But before you cut the vegetables you want to make sure that you wash off the cutting board and the knife so that, again, you don't get sick from the raw chicken that was just on there. //

You cut the green pepper and you want to make sure that you take the core out of the green pepper and cut it into small pieces. // And cut the onion into small pieces. And when you cut the onion you might start crying. // Then you cut the red pepper and it's just like the green pepper—you cut the core out and then you slice it into pieces and then cut it the opposite way into small squares. //

Now you need to add some oil into the pan before you cook the vegetables because the vegetables don't have any fat in them like the chicken does, so if you don't put oil into the pan they will stick to the bottom of the pan. // Then you—now you put the vegetables into the pan and cook them for a few minutes 'til they are slightly crisp and brown. // Now you can add the chicken back into the pan. And also I forgot to mention earlier that you also need to buy a packet of chicken fajita spice mix at the grocery store. // You add that into the pan with the chicken and the vegetables and one cup of water. //

And you put this now onto a lower heat and mix it for a few minutes and the water will thicken up into a nice thick sauce. // You will now take the tortillas and just pop them in the microwave for a minute. // And now take the fajita mixture, put it into a bowl and you can just have a little nice buffet and this should serve five to six people, and it makes a nice dinner. //

EXERCISE 2.3

Big Grandma

DAVID BURNIGHT

Directions

This selection is approximately 4 1/2 minutes long. Find a quiet place to work where you will not be interrupted. Answer study question 1. Find the video selection. Adjust the volume as necessary and be sure you can see the TV monitor clearly. Begin by allowing yourself time to focus on the speaker's face. Record your consecutive interpretation and then answer the study questions.

The passage has brief pauses in it at the places where you rendered the consecutive interpretation but no beep tones. These pauses allow you additional processing time. Do not pause the source tape. If you miss a few words or ideas, resume interpreting again as soon as you can. If you are working into a spoken language, you may either audio- or video-record your interpretation. If you are working into a signed language, use a video recorder to record your interpretation. Answer the study questions and complete the follow-up.

Study Questions

1. Describe the context and participants for this interpretation based on the title of the exercise and the picture of the speaker.

____

____

2. Rate your level of stress during simultaneous interpretation of this passage. Briefly explain your rating.

1	2	3	4	5
No stress	Some	Moderate	High	Very high

____

____

3. Rate your management of processing time. Briefly explain your rating.

1	2	3	4	5
Excellent	Good	Fair	Poor	Nonexistent

____

____

4. Rate your self-monitoring. Briefly explain your rating.

1	2	3	4	5
Excellent	Good	Fair	Poor	Nonexistent

____

____

5. Rate yourself on resuming the interpretation if you faltered. Briefly explain your rating.

1	2	3	4	5
Excellent	Good	Fair	Poor	Nonexistent

____

____

6. Rate your product for accuracy. Briefly explain your rating.

1	2	3	4	5
Excellent	Good	Fair	Poor	Nonexistent

____

____

Transcript for *Big Grandma,* David Burnight

Hi, my name is David Burnight I would like to tell you a little bit about my "Big Grandma." // Some of my favorite memories are about Big Grandma. I call her Big Grandma because I also had a little grandma. // Big Grandma wasn't fat, she was just big. // She grew up in Illinois of pioneer settler stock, and she just had big bones, and was a big woman. // When my mother was 13 Grandpa died, and so Grandma took over and went to work and raised all three children herself. //

When I came along Grandma was living about half the time with our family and half the time with her son, so I always considered her a member of our family. // She would wash dishes and do the ironing, and help my mother a lot, and I enjoyed Big Grandma. //

We had a cabin up in the mountains and would go up every June and grandma would go with us; // and after the sweeping and dusting and bringing down the cobwebs was done, Grandma would go for hikes with me. // She was an old lady, but she was a sturdy old lady. // She always took along a big walking stick, and she told me that it was to kill rattlesnakes with. // She had grown up in a place where the horses grazing on the prairie in Illinois were sometimes bitten by rattlesnakes which would lie in the prairie clover. // And so Grandma hated rattlesnakes and whenever she would see one she would kill it. // And as a matter of fact, when we'd find one on our hikes on the trail, Grandma would beat its head off with her walking stick. //

I think one of the funniest things that happened was one day when my dog Laddie cornered a skunk underneath our cabin. // Wow, what a smell that was! // But Grandma was not even concerned. // That was the day we discovered that Grandma had lost her sense of smell. // And, as a matter of fact now we understood why she'd been complaining lately that food just didn't taste as good as it used to, because when your sense of smell goes you lose your sense of taste, too. //

Grandma had been born in 1860 and she told me that when she was five years old her father took her down to the railway crossing to see President Lincoln's funeral train go by. // To have that kind of living contact with our nation's history always thrilled me when I thought about it. // Grandma lived to be almost 102, and on her 100th birthday President Eisenhower sent her a birthday card. // Of course, he sent birthday cards to every 100-year-old person, but we always thought that it was very special because Grandma was very special to us. //

EXERCISE 2.4

Fusion Cooking

ARLENE FONG CRAIG

Directions

This selection is approximately 6 minutes long. Find a quiet place to work where you will not be interrupted. Answer study question 1. Find the video selection. Adjust the volume as necessary and be sure you can see the TV monitor clearly. Begin by allowing yourself time to focus on the speaker's face. Record your consecutive interpretation and then answer the study questions. The passage has brief pauses in it at the places where you rendered the consecutive interpretation but no beep tones. These pauses allow you additional processing time. Do not pause the source tape. If you miss a few words or ideas, resume interpreting again as soon as you can.

Study Questions

1. Describe the context and participants for this interpretation based on the title of the exercise and the picture of the speaker.

____

____

____

2. Rate your level of stress during simultaneous interpretation of this passage. Briefly explain your rating.

1	2	3	4	5
No stress	Some	Moderate	High	Very high

____

____

3. Rate your management of processing time. Briefly explain your rating.

1	2	3	4	5
Excellent	Good	Fair	Poor	Nonexistent

____

____

____

4. Rate your self-monitoring. Briefly explain your rating.

1	2	3	4	5
Excellent	Good	Fair	Poor	Nonexistent

5. Rate yourself on resuming the interpretation if you faltered. Briefly explain your rating.

1	2	3	4	5
Excellent	Good	Fair	Poor	Nonexistent

6. Rate your product for accuracy. Briefly explain your rating.

1	2	3	4	5
Excellent	Good	Fair	Poor	Nonexistent

Transcript for *Fusion Cooking*, Arlene Fong Craig

Hello. I'm Arlene Fong Craig. There's been a lot of talk lately about "fusion cooking." // But in my opinion, fusion cooking has been happening ever since immigration started. // Any time a people or a culture moves across boundaries, they take other aspects of their culture with them. They keep some things, they discard others, and they transform still others, other items. //

So this is my recipe for fusion Chinese-American roast turkey. You need a 22- to 25-pound turkey, eviscerated, cleaned, and patted dry. //

You'll need, for the marinade, five parts low-sodium soy sauce, four parts of liquor, preferably a good bourbon or Scotch, because the smoky, peaty flavor really blends well with the other flavors of the turkey // and the ingredients, you'll need three parts of mashed or minced garlic and ginger, two parts honey, and one part Asian sesame oil maybe one or two glogs of that. // Combine all of those ingredients and be sure that you thoroughly coat the turkey, both inside and out. //

You'll need to put the turkey in a roasting pan or some other container that is nonreactive, perhaps stainless steel, glass, or a ceramic such as Corningware. // You'll need to marinate the turkey in the refrigerator for at least 24 hours on each side, or if you cannot do that, a half a day on each side. //

When you're ready to roast the turkey, take it out of the refrigerator about an hour beforehand. // Pre-heat the oven about 30 minutes before you're ready to start, to 500°. You'll need a very hot oven in order to sear the bird and to seal in the juices. //

When you're ready to start roasting, place the turkey breast-side down in a non-stick roasting rack, they make Teflon roasting racks, will serve the best, and cover the turkey with an aluminum foil tent. // You can crimp the edges and just loosely cover the back of the bird. And be sure to cover the wing tips and the drumstick ends, also with aluminum foil. //

Roast the turkey, undisturbed, for about 20 minutes—I guarantee it won't burn—and then after 20 minutes, reduce the temperature to 350°. // You'll need to baste the turkey every 15–20 minutes regularly during the cooking time. //

After about two hours for a 25-pound turkey—Oh, I beg your pardon, I forgot: You need, after about an hour, you can remove the aluminum foil tent, and perhaps, the protection from the wing tips and the drumsticks. // Continue basting, and after about two hours, take the turkey out of the oven and flip it over to the breast side. // And the method I've found most useful, after a lot of burned fingers and burned hands, is to take two old but very clean wash cloths, wrap them around your hands, and just insert your hands into the cavities of the bird and flip it over. // And that's really the best and the safest way to turn the turkey over in a whole piece. Be sure to baste it before you put it back into the oven, and to put the tent over the breast, and to protect the wing tips again. //

Continue basting, and after about two hours, give it a test. This is four hours total cooking time. // And if the juices run clear from the thigh, and if, when you press the meat, it does not spring back, then you know the turkey is done. If you like your turkey better more well done, you can leave it in a little longer, but continue to baste the bird. //

As my husband would say, I like my poultry "just done." And he'll say, "Here bird, jump up on the table!" And that's when I know it's ready! //

Be sure you let the turkey rest for 30 minutes for a bird this size before you start carving. In this way, the juices will shrink back into the bird, and the meat will keep its integrity when you begin carving. // So, there you have it: Fusion Chinese-American roast turkey! //

EXERCISE 2.5

My Hobby

JANET PERKIN

Directions

This selection is approximately 6 minutes long. Find a quiet place to work where you will not be interrupted. Answer study question 1. Find the video selection. Adjust the volume as necessary and be sure you can see the TV monitor clearly. Begin by allowing yourself time to focus on the speaker's face.

Record your consecutive interpretation and then answer the study questions. The passage has brief pauses in it at the places where you rendered the consecutive interpretation but no beep tones. These pauses allow you additional processing time. Do not pause the source tape. If you miss a few words or ideas, resume interpreting again as soon as you can.

Study Questions

1. Describe the context and participants for this interpretation based on the title of the exercise and the picture of the speaker.

____

____

____

2. Rate your level of stress during simultaneous interpretation of this passage. Briefly explain your rating.

1	2	3	4	5
No stress	Some	Moderate	High	Very high

____

____

3. Rate your management of processing time. Briefly explain your rating.

1	2	3	4	5
Excellent	Good	Fair	Poor	Nonexistent

____

____

4. Rate your self-monitoring. Briefly explain your rating.

1	2	3	4	5
Excellent	Good	Fair	Poor	Nonexistent

____

____

5. Rate yourself on resuming the interpretation if you faltered. Briefly explain your rating.

1	2	3	4	5
Excellent	Good	Fair	Poor	Nonexistent

6. Rate product for accuracy. Briefly explain your rating.

1	2	3	4	5
Excellent	Good	Fair	Poor	Nonexistent

Transcript for *My Hobby*, Janet Perkin

Hi. My name is Janet Perkin and I'm going to tell you about my hobby, which is antique collecting. // I think this first started when I visited my grandparents' house, which was a 17th century farmhouse on, um, the outskirts of Sheffield. // And we used to visit there every Sunday, and I'm going to tell you what the inside of the house was like compared with what we live in today. // First of all, the kitchen itself had no electricity. // They had to cook on a black, leaded stove, uh, with the heat of coal from the fire. // This was kep—kept gleaming all the time by my grandmother, who polished it regularly. // There was a huge pine table in the kitchen with an old red settle where the farm workers used to come and sit and have their breakfast and lunch. // Also, there was an old stone sink there—we had no running water. They had to go into the garden and draw water from the well. // At nighttime we all had to use a paraffin lamp to heat—to light the room and then a candle we used to take to the bedroom. // In the bedroom we had beautiful pottery jug and water—a water jug to wash with, instead of having the bathroom. //

Later on when my grandparents died I attended the auction. Uh, where, unfortunately, everything was auctioned to the general public and so many of the things were lost to the family. // There's many things I wish I would've been able to have, like the old monk's bench, which was in fact a—a bench which also made into a table. A very rare piece of furniture. // I did manage to collect an old green platter and a gold Noritake coffee set, which I still have today. //

Later on in life I did inherit other pieces from members of the family, such as a grandfather clock from my mother-in-law which had been in the family many, many years. And we still have it today. //

When I was in my late twenties I got the real antique bug and I used to attend many estate sales, auctions, even garage sales. // And throughout the years I've collected a wonderful collection of Victorian, uh, furniture. In fact if you were to enter my living room today you would see a beautiful mahogany sideboard, and on that you would see a beautiful Victorian silver, uh, tea set, coffee pot. And then also in the room you would see a beautiful chaise lounge—for reclining on. // And it's a beautiful room with lots of prints, botanical prints that were popular in Victorian times. //

Now, my family room, which is very, very different, reminds a lot of people of a British pub. // Because you'll see a big fireplace, red brick, with a big oak beam across. Now, on the fireplace there are many, many horse brasses, uh, which are brass lu—uh, good luck charms used on the old farm horses years and years ago. // These adorn the mantelpiece with many brass candlesticks, miner's lamps from the old coal mines and also brass rail lamps. // Now, also in the family room you will find a huge oak table very similar to the one in my grandmother's kitchen. Here is where our family meets every

Sunday evening. // We try and keep the same tradition that we had in my grandmother's time of meeting on Sunday evening and having a family meal together. // In fact you'll also find a beautiful Welsh dresser there with many, many pieces of blue and white china. //

Now today, my children just don't appreciate many of my antiques, but I hope that one day they will, because, uh, these are things that have been treasured through members of the family and through my life, and I hope one day they'll come to love antiques just as I do. //

EXERCISE 2.6

Sailing

CHRIS LEWNES

Directions

This selection is approximately 6 minutes long. Find a quiet place to work where you will not be interrupted. Answer study question 1. Locate this selection on your tape. Adjust the volume as necessary and be sure you can see and hear the TV monitor clearly. Begin by allowing yourself time to focus on the speaker's face. Simultaneously interpret this passage. The passage has brief pauses in it at the places where you rendered the consecutive interpretation but no beep tones. These pauses allow you additional processing time. Do not pause the source tape. If you miss a few words or ideas, resume interpreting again as soon as you can. If you are working into a spoken language, you may either audio- or video-record your interpretation. If you are working into a signed language, use a video recorder to record your interpretation. Answer the remaining study questions and complete the follow-up.

Study Questions

1. Describe the context and participants for this interpretation based on the title of the exercise and the picture of the speaker.

____

____

____

2. Rate your level of stress during simultaneous interpretation of this passage. Briefly explain your rating.

1	2	3	4	5
No stress	Some	Moderate	High	Very high

____

____

3. Rate management of processing time. Briefly explain your rating.

1	2	3	4	5
Excellent	Good	Fair	Poor	Nonexistent

____

____

4. Rate self-monitoring. Briefly explain your rating.

1	2	3	4	5
Excellent	Good	Fair	Poor	Nonexistent

____

____

5. Rate yourself on resuming the interpretation if you faltered. Briefly explain your rating.

1	2	3	4	5
Excellent	Good	Fair	Poor	Nonexistent

____

____

6. Rate your interpretation product for accuracy. Briefly explain your rating.

1	2	3	4	5
Excellent	Good	Fair	Poor	Nonexistent

____

____

Transcript for *Sailing,* Chris Lewnes

Hello. My name is Chris Lewnes. // Today I'd like to talk about my favorite hobby. That's sailing. // Sailing to me is more than just trying to get from one place to another. // I'd like to describe the basic configuration of generally the small boats that I like to sail. //

They're configured as a sloop, which is one mast; // a ketch, two masts; a yawl, also two masts, // however the aft mast is behind the steering wheel; // and a schooner—a schooner has two masts but the aft mast is larger than the forward mast. //

My boat is configured as a sloop // a single mast with a foresail and a mainsail. // In sailing, it's not always point-to-point to get from one place to another. // One has to be aware of the wind, and the direction from which the wind is coming. // In order to get your boat to sail the way you want it to sail you have to be aware of the wind, // and aware of how to trim the sails to get the benefit from the wind to move your boat. //

The best point of sail for a sailboat is with the wind on the beam—90 degrees to the sail. // One can sail all day beautifully that way. // The most difficult way to sail is to get to a point that is upwind; // in other words, if there's an island you'd like to go to here off San Diego. // I like to go to Catalina. // Generally speaking, because of the prevailing wind, // Catalina is directly into the wind from where I want to go. // I can't sail directly there. // So I have to do what's called "tacking." // I've got to sail my boat as efficiently as I can upwind, // which is about 35 degrees to the wind. // I can only get within 35 degrees of the prevailing wind. // So I'll sail as close as I can to 35 degrees // on a course for as long as I think necessary, // and then I'll have to turn to put the boat on the other "tack" as we call it, // with the wind 35 degrees on the other side of the boat. // Therefore the course would look like a zigzag back and forth to my destination. //

Now, depending upon my skill and the layout of the boat // I can perhaps get there quicker than somebody else. // Of course, if somebody else has a better boat and his skills are better, he's gonna beat me there. // That's part of the challenge and the fun of sailing. // Now, we call that sailing uphill. // Of course, just like everything else if you go uphill there's gonna be a reward coming downhill. // Coming back from Catalina, if the wind is the same then it's a beautiful "run" back to San Diego. // A run is with the wind at our back. // So I'll put the sails all the way out, gather as much wind as I can and float effersly—effortlessly back to San Diego. // That's the ideal condition. //

Of course, having skills and being experienced and knowing how to sail enables one to sail in virtually all types of weather, // knowing that, uh, how much your boat can handle; how much wind you can handle; // where to put the sails; how much sail to expose, // how much sail to take in during heavy weather; // are all things that one should know to make sailing pleasurable, safe, and a long-time enjoyable hobby. //

Progress Tracking Sheet

Use this sheet to track your progress with the exercises you have completed. After performing the exercise (one or two times), answering the study questions, and doing the follow-up, fill in the tracking sheet. Note the date that you completed the exercise and give an indication of your level of accomplishment. You can use either a quantitative or a qualitative approach to track your progress.

Exercise Number	Date	First Performance	Study Questions	Follow-up Activity	Questions and Reminders	Date	Second Performance
Exercise 2.1 Quantitative							
Qualitative							
Exercise 2.2 Quantitative							
Qualitative							
Exercise 2.3 Quantitative							
Qualitative							
Quantitative Totals							

Exercise Number	Date	First Performance	Study Questions	Follow-up Activity	Questions and Reminders	Date	Second Performance
Exercise 2.4 Quantitative							
Qualitative							
Exercise 2.5 Quantitative							
Qualitative							
Exercise 2.6 Quantitative							
Qualitative							
Quantitative Totals							

UNIT 3

Sources of Error

Ideally, an interpretation contains no errors. In reality, errors frequently occur in the complex process of simultaneous interpreting. It is important to discuss how errors can occur in the interpreting process and the types of errors that are possible. Errors in the product can be traced to errors or weaknesses in the process. When you gain better control of the interpreting process there will be fewer errors in the product. Accurate skills in monitoring your work help you determine when you need to make corrections in the interpretation. It is important to know which errors are serious and need repairs and the effect of the error on the communication event.

Sources of error in interpreting are observable by examining the product. But by focusing on the product alone we can miss important information about the process. By looking at both the process and the product we can get a clearer picture of where and why errors occur. Gile (1994) describes a process-oriented approach to training in translation that can be applied to interpreting that was developed by the Department of Japanese and Korean Studies of the Institut National des Langues et Civilisations Orientales in Paris. Gile suggests that this process-oriented approach allows for less criticism of the product and greater insight into the process used to create the product. The process-oriented approach allows us to focus on methods used during interpretation. The study questions and follow-up exercises in this book are designed to improve insight into the processes of consecutive interpreting. Improved insight into processes leads to improved product.

By studying the types of errors that interpreters make during simultaneous interpreting we can make inferences about what part of the interpreting process is weak or missing. Although it might seem like a negative approach, error analysis is a well-respected and well-documented way to make inferences about various types of cognitive processes. Error analysis allows us to look at the product of the interpretation and make some assumptions about the process. The goal of error analysis is to improve interpreting processes and, therefore, the product.

The exercises in Units 3–7 in this book provide an opportunity to practice specific skills, answer study questions, and complete the five-step follow-up. Unlike the approach used for the five-step follow-up in *The Effective Interpreting Series: Consecutive Interpreting from English,* which allowed a more detailed analysis of errors, here you will use an approach that is more streamlined. The five-step follow-up is described in detail in the Introduction and summarized here.

Review your entire interpretation. Select the portion (this part will vary in length from 1 to 3 minutes) that you would like to analyze and revise. You will analyze only this portion of your work. You will use the steps below to revise each error that you identify.

List at least one positive aspect of your interpretation.

Step 1 **Interpretation Rendered**

Transcribe only the portion of the interpretation you would like to improve.

Step 2 **Determine Underlying Reason**

Although there are many possible reasons for errors in interpretation, in this analysis you will select from one of the following for each error identified in Step 1.

Comprehension

Transfer

Reformulation

Step 3 **Probable Effect of Error on Communicative Function**

After selecting the type of error, rate the error according to how it impacts the communication, keeping in mind that not all errors are equally serious.

5 = No negative consequences to participants

4 = Consequence of errors is minimal

3 = Consequence of errors is moderate

2 = Consequence of errors is severe

1 = Consequence of errors is grave

Step 4 **Revisions**

Write, and then later record, a revised interpretation that better preserves the meaning of the original source message.

Step 5 **Action Plan for Improvement**

Once you have determined the type of error and its impact, write down what action you plan to take to improve your work. For example, you can decide to focus on comprehension and review the material until you are certain you have fully understood the message, or you can re-record your interpretation to create an improved product.

____

____

____

____

In this book you will be using a combination of some of the features of the five-step follow-up that have appeared in earlier volumes in *The Effective Interpreting Series*. It is necessary to move to a more streamlined approach to evaluating your work because the simultaneous interpreting process itself is so demanding. When you use the five-step follow-up you are analyzing your work after it is completed. You will also be learning to monitor and correct your work in real time while simultaneously interpreting, when a detailed error analysis process is not possible.

Gonzales et al. (1991) describe an important study of categories of interpreter errors. Ten years of data collection on simultaneous interpreting in legal settings formed the basis for this study. The results of the study support what many interpreter educators have intuitively "felt" but could not explain. Interpreters can usually identify when an interpretation is weak but may have difficulty describing why. This unit summarizes causes of errors, effect of location of errors, and types of errors. According to Gonzales et al. there are eight broad areas of errors. They are literal translations, inadequate language proficiency, errors in register conservation, distortion, omission, added information, protocol, procedure and ethics, and non-conservation of paralinguistic elements. Some of these are summarized below.

Causes of Interpretation Errors

Inadequate Language Proficiency

Language proficiency in two or more languages should precede interpreter training. The Gonzalez et al. data support the notion that inadequate language proficiency in the source language, target language, or both is the most frequent source of interpreter error. "General lack of language fluency makes it impossible for an interpreter to comprehend text well enough to convert ideas fully and faithfully at the requisite speed into the TL without reliance on glossaries and dictionaries and without faltering and communication breakdowns " (Gonzalez et al., 1991, p.282). Inadequate language proficiency can lead to a variety of types of errors. For a review of language proficiency skills in English see *The Effective Interpreting Series: English Skills Development*. Some of the error types explained below are due to language proficiency problems and some are due to weaknesses in the interpretation processes. Inadequate language proficiency can create problems in all other areas within the interpreting process. Language proficiency in both languages is an essential prerequisite to the development of interpreting skills.

Processing Problems

These authors say that problems in language proficiency lead to four problems in processing. One problem is the lack of ability to correctly predict language patterns. For example, in English a common pattern for opening a speech is "Good evening ladies and gentlemen". We generally do not hear "Good evening gentlemen and ladies." In addition to usual patterns of how sentences and expressions are constructed, language patterns are also revealed in intonation patterns. Interpreters need to know that the intonation of the speaker indicates that a list is to be given next or that the speech is about to conclude. When the speaker says, "The following reasons tell us why..." the interpreter mentally prepares for a list. Likewise, a phrase like "In conclusion..." lets the interpreter know that the speaker is about to conclude remarks. This allows the interpreter to prepare for a summary statement. When the interpreter realizes this, he or she can mentally re-inspect the content of the speech to access memory related to the points made so far.

A second category is cognitive processing errors. This type of error can be attributed to weaknesses in such skills as comprehension, memory, acuity and discrimination, repetition, number processing, and multi-tasking. For a review of these skills see *The Effective Interpreting Series: Cognitive Processing in English*.

The third category described by Gonzales et al. is inadequate attention span in the weaker language due to a misuse of effort at the comprehension and memory storage stage of the interpreting process. It is a common experience to feel fatigue in listening to and trying to comprehend a language in which you are not completely fluent. When intralingual abilities in the weaker language improve, less attention and effort are required to listen, comprehend, and remember. Inadequate attention span will lead to errors in interpretation because the interpreter cannot fully and correctly remember information that requires a proportionately greater share of the cognitive effort. A weakness in attention span in the weaker language could affect comprehension of the source message if the source language is the weaker language. Alternatively, if the target language is the weaker language, then weaknesses in attention span will lead to errors in monitoring and self-correction.

The fourth problem is interference between languages. This means that sounds, words, grammatical patterns, and other features from one language are incorrectly used in the other language. Gonzalez et al. conclude that language proficiency will affect the speed and accuracy of the interpretation. They suggest that there are two main types of errors: grammatical and lexical.

Location of Error

The location of the error often determines the level of seriousness of the error. Using a three-phase model allows us to note the effect of errors quickly. The three phases are comprehension, transfer, and reformulation. If the error occurs in comprehension, the first phase of the interpretation process, it is a more serious error than if it occurs later in the process. Errors in comprehension will prevent the interpreter from understanding the message well enough to move on to another phase of the process. If the error occurs in the transfer phase, it indicates that the interpreter understood but had weaknesses in transferring the message. Errors in reformulation indicate that the interpreter understood and could transfer the message, but made errors in expression that could include pronunciation errors or other errors that are less likely to have a negative impact on the communication event.

Types of Errors

Literal Translation

The first error category Gonzales et al. describe is literal translation. This means that the interpreter does not preserve the ideas but focuses on substituting words from the target language for words in the source language. This substitution approach creates grammatical errors in the target language. The example below is from one of the transcripts that Gonzalez et al. studied (p.282). It shows how literal translation can distort the message. As the authors point out, a single error like this is not too grave, but if it is repeated and combined with errors of this and other types, the message of the speaker will be skewed.

Interpreter: I work in the package of lemons.

Should be: I'm a lemon packer.

Although Gonzales' examples pertain to Spanish–English interpretation, we can generalize these types of errors to other language pairs. In interpreting from English to ASL, using ASL signs in English syntax creates a literal approach that often distorts the message. One way to check your work to see whether your interpretation follows English syntax is to analyze your interpretation and study the word order. If the word order of your interpretation follows the word order patterns of the source language instead of the target language, it is likely that the message will be skewed. Literal translation errors can be due to inadequate language proficiency or to inadequate preparation in interpreting procedures.

Lexical Errors

Errors at the lexical level or word level are due to a weak or inadequate access to a wide variety of synonyms and other intralingual skills. Gonzalez et al. say,

"Accurate interpreting results from a combination of lexical precision and highly developed performance skills" (p. 284). The results of a national exam for court interpreters show that in 1989, nearly 40% of those who failed did so because of weaknesses in vocabulary. For example, an interpreter said "Nowadays a lot of people reappear dead" when the interpreter should have said "Nowadays a lot of people turn up dead." (p.284). Weaknesses in target language vocabulary can be overcome by accurate paraphrasing skills. With accurate and rapid paraphrasing skills the interpreter can explain the topic or term in different words even when they do not know the specific term in the target language. Gonzalez et al. point out that lexical weaknesses cause errors and can lead to a total breakdown in the interpretation process. This means that in legal settings important parts of the testimony may not be interpreted correctly or at all. In still other cases, interpreters invent terminology in order to keep going. "Language deficient interpreters, like second language learners, rely on false cognates or invent words in order to express the meaning for which they have no lexicon available" (p. 285). This is the case for spoken and signed language interpreters alike. In either case the results can be disastrous because the meaning is lost.

Errors in Register Conservation

Gonzales et al. say that register refers to the level of formality of speech. This category is especially important in the courtroom where there may be a variety of types of speech, from very formal to very informal. Register conservation is important in other settings as well. For example, if the interpreter has command of only a very informal register, the interpreter's work will only be accurate in that register and skewed in all other registers. Gonzalez et al. point out that the problem includes being able to correctly understand a full range of registers and then being able to find the appropriate expression in the target language while preserving the register. The authors give an example from the results of a national test for interpreters. The idiom "scared to death" was correctly interpreted by only 28% of the 222 people who took the test in 1988. Some of the incorrect interpretations included the following utterances.

She is afraid of death.

She can't sleep at night.

She is very afraid of her death.

In all of these examples, the meaning is not preserved and the impact of the testimony is lost. Gonzales et al. stress repeatedly that linguistic flexibility is absolutely essential for interpreters. Linguistic flexibility is especially important when the speaker repeats him or herself and uses idiomatic language because in that case the interpreter must have a variety of ways to express the same idea.

Omission

Another common error in Gonzalez et al.'s taxonomy of errors is information that is deleted or left out. When experienced interpreters leave out information it tends to be due to fatigue. In less experienced interpreters, omissions tend to be due to failure to comprehend or inability to express a concept in the target language or other language- based problems. Processing or memory problems can lead to omissions.

Gonzalez et al. say that omissions can confuse witnesses in legal settings. This confusion arises because the interpreter omits part of the witnesses' response and then the question is repeated to the witness. The witness thinks that elaboration is requested, not repetition, and confusion increases. Here are some examples of omissions from the data Gonzalez et al. collected. The underlined portions indicate omissions.

> **Interpreter:** She said that when they came in she got nervous, that she was very nervous. She asked what's happening and when she asked that and got in front of them, they put her aside.
>
> **Should be:** Well, when they entered, she says she got scared and became very nervous. When she asked them what was happening and faced them, they took her aside and beat her up.
>
> **Interpreter:** Well, they didn't kill him, they threw him in there.
>
> **Should be:** Well, they didn't kill him, they threw him in there alive.

Additions

According to Gonzalez et al., additions can occur for several reasons. When the interpreter does not understand the source message, he or she may use several possible meanings to express the concept. Sometimes interpreters use silence inappropriately by adding repetitions and fillers that are not part of the message in hopes of clarifying the interpretation. Added information and repetition can change a concise and compelling answer into a rambling and weak response. The users of the interpreting service will not know that the original answer was concise and compelling. Gonzalez et al. cite Berk-Seligson (1987), who demonstrated that "powerless' speech is characterized by lengthened responses. A response that is perceived as powerless can disadvantage the participants, even if the actual response was concise and powerful. Using additions and fillers during silence not only weakens and distorts the interpretation, but also prevents the interpreter from using the silence as a brief rest period.

Here are some examples from Gonzales et al.'s data. The underlined portions indicate additions.

> **Interpreter:** *I believed* that they killed, and it was *an injustice what they did to her.*
>
> **Should be:** . . . that they killed her unjustly.
>
> **Interpreter:** I have no idea.
>
> **Should be:** I don't know.

"This not only lengthens the speaker's response, but shifts it into another attitude posture, which does not replicate stylistically the speaker's intention."

Protocol, Procedures, and Ethics

This part of Gonzalez et al.'s taxonomy addresses the importance of protocol, procedures, and ethics in the interpreting situation. Errors in any of these three areas can be as damaging to the message as any of the previous categories. One aspect of this part of the taxonomy is the importance of the interpreter being faithful to the message even when the message includes profanities. A second aspect of this category is the necessity to correct errors, especially when the interpretation becomes part of a formal record. Some interpreters working in legal settings have not been trained to correct the court record and some potentially damaging errors remain and can cause confusion and harm. Other people in legal (and other) settings often do not know the interpreter's role, so the interpreter must be able to explain the role of the interpreter in a concise and effective manner. Sometimes interpreters themselves do not understand their own role and converse with participants when they should not. Conversing with a witness while waiting for a trial to begin may provide the interpreter with additional information that may later bias the interpretation or lead to mistakes.

Non-Conservation of Paralinguistic Elements, Hedges, and Fillers

The final category of the taxonomy is non-conservation of paralinguistic elements, hedges, and fillers. Gonzalez et al. say that this kind of error occurs in the work of developing and new interpreters. Filtering out this kind of speech changes the impact of the testimony. Here is an example from the data.

Interpreter: Well, uh, because it is that way. Let's put it this way . . .

Should be: Well, uh, I don't know how to say it. It's that when . . . no, of course it was that way, but how can I tell you: Let's see, let's see, let's put it this way...

By understanding the causes of errors, the effect of location of errors, and types of errors that can occur in interpreting you can improve your overall interpretation and the self-correction process, when needed. The exercises in this unit encourage you to keep the factors related to errors in mind and to notice how errors impact your interpretations. As you practice interpreting these selections you will create a product and then answer questions about your interpretations. If you are working into a signed language, record your interpretation on videotape for analysis. If you are working into a spoken language you can use either a video or audio recorder.

EXERCISES IN SOURCES OF ERROR

EXERCISE 3.1

Introduction

JAIME CORONADO

Directions

This selection is approximately 1 minute long. Find a quiet place to work where you will not be interrupted. Answer study question 1. Find the video selection. Adjust the volume as necessary and be sure you can see the TV monitor clearly. Begin by allowing yourself time to focus on the speaker's face. Read the transcript once and then simultaneously interpret the selection. Do not pause or rewind the videotape. Answer the remaining study questions and complete the follow-up.

Study Questions

1. Describe context and participants for this interpretation based on the exercise title and picture of the speaker.

____

____

2. List five of the possible types of errors discussed in this unit and provide a brief description of each.

____

____

____

____

____

____

____

3. Were you aware of any processing problems such as predicting language patterns or remembering what you heard? Refer to the transcript and underline any portions of the text where you feel these types of errors occurred.

4. Compare source and target messages to examine your interpretation for examples of literal translation. If you find examples of literal translation, put parentheses around the corresponding sections of the transcript. Examine your work for examples of omissions. Refer to the transcript and underline any information that is omitted in your interpretation.

5. Why do errors in comprehension tend to be more serious than errors in reformulation or expression? Compare source and target messages to examine your interpretation for errors in comprehension. If you find errors in comprehension mark a "C" on the transcript in the corresponding location.

Transcript for *Introduction,* Jaime Coronado

Hi. My name is Jaime Coronado. I am originally from Chicago, Illinois. For the past 14 years, I have been living in Washington, D.C. and working as a sign language interpreter. I went to Waubonsee Community College in Sugar Grove, Illinois, and trained as an interpreter there, then moved out here those 14 years ago. Right now, presently, I'm working at the United States Capitol. I work for the Congressional Special Services. I am an official employee of the United States Senate. My responsibilities include interpreting for members of Congress, the United States Senate, and their constituents.

Five-Step Follow-up

Write at least one positive aspect of your interpretation.

____

Step 1 **Interpretation Rendered**

Review your entire interpretation. Select the portion that reflects your best work. Transcribe only the portions of the interpretation you would like to improve. You do not need to transcribe the source text. Use the steps outlined below to revise each error that you identify.

____

____

____

____

Step 2 **Determine Underlying Reason**

Although there are many possible reasons for errors in interpretation, in this analysis you will select one of the following for each error you identified in Step 1.

Comprehension

Transfer

Reformulation

____

____

____

____

Step 3 **Probable Effect of Error on Communicative Function**

After selecting the type of error, rate each error according to how it impacts the communication, keeping in mind that not all errors are equally serious.

5 = No negative consequences to participants

4 = Consequence of errors is minimal

3 = Consequence of errors is moderate

2 = Consequence of errors is severe

1 = Consequence of errors is grave

Step 4 **Revisions**

Write, and then later record, a revised interpretation for each error that better preserves the meaning of the original source message.

Step 5 **Action Plan for Improvement**

Once you have determined the types of errors and their impact, write down what action you plan to take to improve your work.

EXERCISE 3.2

Childhood Mischief

MARQUESSA BROWN

Directions

This selection is approximately 4 1/2 minutes long. Find a quiet place to work where you will not be interrupted. Answer study question 1. Find the video selection. Adjust the volume as necessary and be sure you can see the TV monitor clearly. Begin by allowing yourself time to focus on the speaker's face. Read the transcript once and then simultaneously interpret the selection. Do not pause or rewind the videotape. Answer the remining study questions and complete the follow-up.

Study Questions

1. Describe context and participants for this interpretation based on the exercise title and picture of the speaker.

   ____

   ____

   ____

2. Did your proficiency in the source language affect your ability to interpret this passage? If yes, explain why. Did your proficiency in the target language affect your ability to interpret this passage? If yes, explain why.

   ____

   ____

   ____

3. During the interpretation process, were you aware of any processing problems such as predicting language patterns or remembering what you heard? Refer to the transcript and underline any portions of the text where you feel these types of errors occurred.

   ____

   ____

   ____

4. Compare source and target messages to examine your interpretation for examples of literal translation. If you find examples of literal translation, put parentheses around the corresponding sections of the transcript. Examine your work for examples of omissions. Refer to the transcript and underline any information that is omitted in your interpretation.

5. Compare source and target messages to examine your interpretation for errors in comprehension. If you find errors in comprehension mark a "C" on the transcript in the corresponding location.

Transcript for *Childhood Mischief,* Marquessa Brown

Hi. My name's Marquessa. I'm going to share something very interesting and, at the same time, kind of funny. It's about something that happened to me when I was, I believe, about 7 years old. I was a very, very active kid, always getting into things. Whenever my parents would want to punish me, I would run. I'd hide. I'd get under chairs. I'd get under beds. I'd go anyplace to keep my parents from finding me when they wanted to punish me. I have a younger brother, who's 2-1/2 years younger than me, and I think when he was born, I was one of the 2-1/2 year olds who didn't take very well to having this new person coming into the household, and there was clearly some sibling rivalry as I was growing up. So as we grew up, I was always kind of picking on my brother. I always picked on him. I would always hit him, I would always make him cry. I would always take his things away from him. I was always getting punished for doing something, and I would hide so they couldn't find me to punish me. Sometimes, my parents would make me go to my room for things that I had done. And I would go in my room, and I would yell out the window to everyone who passed by, "Hi. My parents put me in my room. They're punishing me for something that I did." Sometimes, I would go in the bathroom, and I would get my dad's razor, and I would decide I wanted to shave. And so I would shave with my dad's razor, and I would cut my face all up. So I was a very, very active kid.

I think the most exciting part, which I've been trying to get to for a few minutes, was the time I got my head stuck under the steps. I used to put—and this was outside. Sometimes, I would go outside, and I'd play, and I'd take my mom's pots and pans out of the kitchen. And I'd find big rocks, and I would put those in the pot, so those would be my roast. And then I would go and I would find grass and all kinds of things, and I would put those in the smaller pots, and those would be my vegetables. And then, I'd find some smaller rocks and put them in another pot, and those would be my potatoes. And then I would mix some mud with water, and that would be my gravy over my roast in the big pot. And then, you know, I'd take some more mud and mix it in with the rocks, and that, with the smaller rocks, and that would be my gravy over my potatoes. Well, this one day when I was out there playing, the big rock that I needed for my roast was under the steps. I was trying to figure out how am I going to get this rock from under the steps. So, I took my head, and I put it under the steps, and I said, "Ah, there's the rock! I've got it." So I had my hands on the rock. I'm under there. I lift the rock up. And I can't get my head out. It's stuck! And I'm trying to get my head, and I'm wiggling, and I'm wiggling. And you would think a 6-year-old's head would not be so big that they couldn't get it from under these steps. I'm yelling, and I'm wiggling, and I'm trying to get from under the steps. It felt like ever. I never got my head from under the steps! So I had to wait for my mom to come looking for me, and she found me with my head stuck under the steps. I'm crying, and I'm saying, "Mommy, help, I can't get out." My mom is trying to get my head from under the steps. And by this time, I'm just so panicked. And she's panicked because she can't get my head out.

So, there I am stuck under those steps. So then, my mom calls a neighbor, who comes over. And between the two of them, they get me out of the steps. Well, you would think that my mother would be so scared that she would not have fussed at me. As usual, I got fussed at for doing something else I had no business doing. And in addition to being fussed at because I had my head stuck under the steps trying to get this rock for my roast, my mother saw all of her pots and pans outside. And she was furious, because I had taken her pots and pans, and I had mud and rocks in one and weeds, and grass, and all kinds of things in another one. So that's kind of the story, the most special thing that happened to me.

Five-Step Follow-up

Write at least one positive aspect of your interpretation.

___

Step 1 **Interpretation Rendered**

Review your entire interpretation. Select the 3-minute portion that reflects your best work. Transcribe only the portions of the interpretation you would like to improve. You do not need to transcribe the source text. Use the steps outlined below to revise each error that you identify.

___

___

___

Step 2 **Determine Underlying Reason**

Although there are many possible reasons for errors in interpretation, in this analysis you will select one of the following for each error identified in Step 1.

Comprehension

Transfer

Reformulation

___

___

Step 3 **Probable Effect of Error on Communicative Function**

After selecting the types of errors, rate each error according to how it impacts the communication, keeping in mind that not all errors are equally serious.

5 = No negative consequences to participants

4 = Consequence of errors is minimal

3 = Consequence of errors is moderate

2 = Consequence of errors is severe

1 = Consequence of errors is grave

Step 4 **Revisions**

Write, and then later record, a revised interpretation for each error that better preserves the meaning of the original source message.

Step 5 **Action Plan for Improvement**

Once you have determined the types of errors and their impact, write down what action you plan to take to improve your work.

EXERCISE 3.3

Creating Good Assignments

LESLIE RACH

Directions

This selection is approximately 9 minutes long. Find a quiet place to work where you will not be interrupted. Answer study question 1. Find the video selection. Adjust the volume as necessary and be sure you can see the TV monitor clearly. Begin by allowing yourself time to focus on the speaker's face. Read the transcript once and then simultaneously interpret the selection. Do not pause or rewind the videotape. Answer the remaining study questions and complete the follow-up.

Study Questions

1. Describe context and participants for this interpretation based on the exercise title and picture of the speaker.

2. Did your proficiency in the source language affect your ability to interpret this passage? If yes, explain why. Did your proficiency in the target language affect your ability to interpret this passage? If yes, explain why.

3. During the interpretation process, were you aware of any processing problems such as predicting language patterns or remembering what you heard? Refer to the transcript and underline any portions of the text where you feel these types of errors occurred.

4. Compare source and target messages to examine your interpretation for examples of literal translation. If you find examples of literal translation, put parentheses around the corresponding sections of the transcript. Examine your work for examples of omissions. Refer to the transcript and underline any information that is omitted in your interpretation.

5. Compare source and target messages to examine your interpretation for errors in comprehension. If you find errors in comprehension mark a "C" on the transcript in the corresponding location.

Transcript for *Creating Good Assignments*, Leslie Rach

Hi there. I'm Leslie Rach, and I'm going to talk about creating reading, writing, and research assignments for students in English classes. And it also has application for people who are teaching content area courses, courses such as psychology, sociology, biology, physics, any of the courses on the college level. And you could even try this with high school or middle school students. The key is to think about your reading and writing assignments as something that will involve content. And I think that's one thing that teachers often have a hard time with. You kind of want your students to write, and you want your students to read, but you end up kind of giving them a mixed bag of reading assignments that don't have any real coherence or any sort of theme. So I like to think about giving my students assignments that are related to a particular content area. And I'm gonna use two examples to illustrate how you could do this on very different levels.

First of all, I teach a class that is more of a skills-based class, and it's for freshman students in college. And it's a reading comprehension class, theoretically. Now, I do like to integrate some writing assignments. And, so, I do this by creating some mini research projects. And one of these research projects is to have students read something from our textbook, our regular reading skills textbook, and then to go find an article in the library. And I have them use the computer system in the library instead of looking on the web, even though I know the web is the way of the future. I'm a little old-fashioned, and I like for them to actually go look in journals, newspapers, and magazines. Also, some of the information you get on the web is secondhand, and it tends to be a little watered down. And students really need to be more exposed to firsthand information and to realize that there is quality information on some of these issues that they're reading about in their books, that there are real issues that people are writing about other than textbook authors. So, that being said, I send them off to the library, and I ask them to look for an issue that came up in the reading that we were doing, so that they're getting exposure to the textbook writing and then writing from a journal, or a periodical, or some such source. And then they assemble their sources. So, students usually come to class with an article that they've researched on the topic, and then I have all of the students write the name of the article and the main idea from the article on the blackboards in the classroom: the author's name, volume number, other things like that that might be pertinent for other students who would be interested in looking up the same article, because often, students see a topic and then they decide they want to work on that topic. So, there's a little information sharing in the beginning.

So, students come in. They write the name of the article, the main idea, whatnot, on the board, and then everyone browses around at these different issues that have been brought to class, and they decide on their research project that they're going to do related to that topic. And, that the activity that I just described really involves a lot of skill. I mean, you know, we're teaching students how to find and write main-idea statements. And there's the activity that kind of brings it into practice in a sort of academic way, instead of just reading a paragraph and writing down the main idea. Now, they're doing it to do a real research project.

So, they look at these titles and main ideas, and then they go off and start their own research project. And you can really arrange this however you'd like. I usually have students practice the skills that I'm working on in class, like concept mapping. Maybe they'll go find the article, draw a concept map of that article, which means any number of things. It could be a timeline; it could be clustering. It depends on what the pattern of organization was in that reading that they were doing. And often, it's a combination of patterns, which is good for them to see as well. So, they draw a concept map, maybe write a summary. And here, they're bringing in all the skills that they've learned in class. And then, the real key, where they start to do some serious research, and even though it's on a very fundamental level, it's really beneficial for them, because we do it as scholars on all levels, all the way up to doctoral dissertations, masters thesis, and whatnot, even writing papers for presentations, is to bring the information from the different sources into one cohesive piece at the end. So, it's sort of like writing a little literature review, if you will. Certainly not like a masters thesis, but it's a start. So, students are always tempted to summarize the article, summarize the article, and then is their report, again, write another summary of the articles. But what I encourage them to do is look for the issues in the article. So, for example, if you have two articles on smoking cessation programs, and you find out that, wow, the patch keeps coming up again and again. Well, maybe that should be a heading in your report, and under that you can put both of the articles' information on that issue. And so, they start to think about discourse communities, and how writers respond to each other, and how writers are writing to create a body of knowledge. And then they become writers creating a new body of knowledge with their report. So, even, you know, just thinking about using that with freshman students on a skills level, you really get some kind of interesting projects. And so, that's one thing I like to do with this reading class that I teach.

And I have one more example that I use with a more advanced class. These tend to be sophomore students, thinking about deciding on a major for their academic career. And I'm teaching a similar class, a reading class, but the needs are very different. So, again, the goal is to integrate reading, writing, and research projects in a meaningful way for my students. So what I do with this class is I have four content areas that I determined by random really. I just decide which ones I'm going to do the beginning of that semester. And in the past, I've done biology, sociology, psychology, literature, history. And I arrange my course syllabus into those sections, with equal amount of time devoted to each one; say, three weeks for each section. And then I have a guest speaker come to class from each of those areas and do a little mini lecture on some important content that they determine on their own from their area. It could be—one time, I had a gentleman talk about—he's doing child psychology—so he decided to talk about Erikson's stages of development. And that was really perfect, because it was contained in a one-hour lecture, and it gave the students some content, which they could then apply to their research projects. So, in that three-week period after his lecture, we did all kinds of different research, reading, and writing assignments, which then culminated in a short research paper, about 10, 7- to 10-page research paper. And doing that paper, they learned all kinds of things. They learned how psychologists talk about different issues in the area. They learned more in-depth about the theory, Erikson's theory. They learned how psychologists write, how psychologists think. They learned about writing the psychology paper APA style, and how to put the paper together, write an abstract, and the different section of the paper, how it should be arranged. And they did this, like I said, for five different content areas. So, students then, when they went off to their major courses, they knew MLA style; they knew CBE style from biology. They knew APA style. They knew how to arrange papers in the content areas. And I think that was a really beneficial course for students who were thinking about becoming academics. And, like I said, these are just two examples of how you can create reading, writing, and research projects for your students at all levels, and to add some content to what would otherwise be sort of vacuous English courses.

Five-Step Follow-up

Write at least one positive aspect of your interpretation.

Step 1 **Interpretation Rendered**

Review your entire interpretation. Select the 3-minute portion that reflects your best work. Transcribe only the portions of the interpretation you would like to improve. You do not need to transcribe the source text. Use the steps outlined below to revise each error that you identify.

____

____

____

____

Step 2 **Determine Underlying Reason**

Although there are many possible reasons for errors in interpretation, in this analysis you will select one of the following for each error identified in Step 1.

Comprehension

Transfer

Reformulation

____

____

____

Step 3 **Probable Effect of Error on Communicative Function**

After selecting the types of errors, rate each error according to how it impacts the communication, keeping in mind that not all errors are equally serious.

5 = No negative consequences to participants

4 = Consequence of errors is minimal

3 = Consequence of errors is moderate

2 = Consequence of errors is severe

1 = Consequence of errors is grave

____

____

____

Step 4 **Revisions**

Write, and then later record, a revised interpretation for each error that better preserves the meaning of the original source message.

____

____

____

____

Step 5 **Action Plan for Improvement**

Once you have determined the types of errors and their impact, write down what action you plan to take to improve your work.

____

____

____

Progress Tracking Sheet

Use this sheet to track your progress with the exercises you have completed. After performing the exercise (one or two times), answering the study questions, and doing the follow-up, fill in the tracking sheet. Note the date that you completed the exercise and give an indication of your level of accomplishment. You can use either a quantitative or a qualitative approach to track your progress.

Exercise Number	Date	First Performance	Study Questions	Follow-up Activity	Questions and Reminders	Date	Second Performance
Exercise 3.1 Quantitative							
Qualitative							
Exercise 3.2 Quantitative							
Qualitative							
Exercise 3.3 Quantitative							
Qualitative							
Quantitative Totals							

UNIT 4

Comprehension

This text uses a broad three-part framework for simultaneous interpreting that includes comprehension, transfer, and reformulation. This simple framework streamlines learning activities that lead to the development of simultaneous interpreting skills. In reality, simultaneous interpreting includes many more than three cognitive operations. The remaining units in this text explore each of these three broad areas in more depth.

Comprehension is the first broad area in the interpreting process. This is the stage that allows the interpreter to perceive and decipher the message. According to Massaro and Shlesinger (1979), "Perceivers use multiple sources of information to make sense of the message. Bottom-up and top-down approaches are used to arrive at the most appropriate interpretation" (p. 21). This means that you understand information by using two different approaches simultaneously. You use the context and background knowledge (top-down) in combination with new facts that you piece together (bottom-up). Massaro and Shlesinger say that the interpreter must work to understand more than just linguistic information. The emotional and paralinguistic information is an essential part of the message and must be correctly perceived and processed by the interpreter at the comprehension phase. For example, if the interpreter misunderstands the emotional content of a message that is meant to be sarcastic and understands it as a compliment, the resulting interpretation will be skewed.

Perceiving the source message is really a larger issue than simply understanding the linguistic message in the source language. The interpreter must also attend to paralinguistic information such as that conveyed by inflection of the message, whether it is signed or spoken, the facial expression of the speaker, the context in which the message is being delivered, and to whom it is being delivered. The interpreter must keep the emotional impact or illocutionary force of the message preserved in order to deliver an accurate message.

Comprehension of source material (linguistic and paralinguistic) is an essential skill that underlies all other skills in the interpretation process. According to Gile (1995), linguistic comprehension is based on two essential features. One is knowledge of words in a language and the other is knowledge of the grammar of a language. Yet, these two features are not enough to ensure comprehension. The context in which the words and grammar are used must be taken into consideration.

The comprehension process generally begins with a message in the source language. When this message is sent to a receiver and understood in the target language (TL) by that receiver, basic communication is thought to have occurred. This description is too simple, because as Gile points out, each listener's prior knowledge, knowledge of the vocabulary, grammar, culture, and context will influence understanding. The more information or ELK a person has, the more likely they are to be able to understand the message as intended by the sender. The process of communication via an interpreter is more complicated than when two people who share the same language are communicating with each other. During interpretation the source language message is sent to and received by the interpreter. The interpreter must understand the meaning of the source language message, interpret the message, and give that message expression in another language, the TL. The person who receives the interpreted message ideally understands the message as intended by the original sender of the message, but there is no foolproof way to measure this understanding.

Gile (1995) devotes an entire chapter to the importance of comprehension in the interpretation process in his book entitled *Basic Concepts and Models for Interpreter and Translator Training*. He stresses that the interpreter's need for ELK never levels off, but rather increases. Next, he stresses the importance of "deliberate and sustained analysis" (p. 85) as a way to improve comprehension. The process of sustained analysis is an ongoing process of listening intently and checking probable meanings with the current context to see whether these make sense and whether these probable meanings are likely to be the meanings intended by the speaker. Another important point that Gile makes is that the type of understanding or comprehension that the interpreter must use is not the same as that used by a layperson. The interpreter must constantly listen and analyze the incoming message. When you do the exercises in this unit make a conscious effort to use deliberate and sustained analysis as you listen.

Gonzalez et al. (1991) say, "To be able to process the source language message accurately, the interpreter must be able to listen effectively and to attend to meaning" (p. 380). According to Weaver (1972, in Gonzalez 1991), there are at least three important types of processing that are related to listening.

(1) identifying the meaning units in the message, (2) identifying the speaker's intent, and (3) calling appropriate ELK or context into play to help frame the information.

Jones (1998) explains how important analysis is for the interpreter. "The better their understanding and analysis, the better placed they are to express themselves freely, using their own words while respecting the content of the original. Provided the same ideas are being expressed and the same relations between those ideas, the interpreter can invert the order of two sentences, merge two of the speaker's sentences into one or on the contrary divide one long sentence into a number of shorter ones" (p. 41).

When working from L2 into L1 it is especially important to focus your listening skills on the incoming message. "Abbott et al. (1981) note that when people listen to a message in a language other than their native tongue, it takes them longer to process the information, they are more likely to make mistakes in comprehension, it is more difficult to predict outcome, and their memory is more heavily taxed and therefore works less efficiently" (Gonzalez et al. 1991, p.381).

Main Idea Identification

Another indication of careful listening and accurate analysis is the ability to find and state the main idea of a text. Sometimes the main idea is also called the gist of the text or macroprocessing. The term "main idea" means the central premise around which the rest of the ideas are expanded. The supporting ideas are those that help expand the main idea. When the main idea is altered or deleted, the meaning of the text changes. The main idea contains important information. Supporting ideas add information to the main idea and make it clearer and stronger. The supporting ideas or details are less important to the overall theme than the main idea. If supporting ideas are omitted, the overall main idea is not likely to be changed substantially. When main ideas and supporting ideas are included in an interpretation the ideas should maintain the same relative importance with respect to each other. The ability to use macroprocessing indicates that the interpreter is able to see beyond the details and process the message at an overall level. When an interpreter can do this he or she tends to use less energy because it allows him or her to process the segments of the message that are most salient and avoid getting lost in the details.

The main idea can be summarized into a topic sentence. Sometimes the topic sentence is further abbreviated into a title. The main idea is sometimes stated early in the speech and then referred to again and again until the topic is changed. Once the main idea is stated, it becomes implicit or understood in the ideas that follow it. Ideas presented after the main idea can be points that clarify or support the main idea.

Cunningham and Moore (1986) suggest that one factor that determines what a person selects as the main idea is what captures their attention.

These authors deal primarily with finding the main idea in written materials, rather than spoken, but the same principles can apply to finding the main point of spoken material or written material. The interpreter is not listening to gain information for his or her own personal use and so may focus more on the speaker's purpose. The type of listening needed in interpreting is more focused than the type of listening generally done for personal listening. However, as Cunningham and Moore point out, the writer or speaker's purpose may not always be easy to find. For example, sometimes the speaker says he or she will discuss a certain topic but the remarks do not pertain to the subject.

Interpreters must be able to distinguish main from supporting ideas in order to prioritize the important points and to make quick decisions about which points are main ideas and which points support the main idea. In order to be able to identify the main idea, you must sort the ideas by level of importance and then by topic. This is accomplished by using a specific type of analytical thinking called hierarchical thinking. A hierarchy is a rank ordering or arranging of things in order of importance. In a well-organized speech or talk, the main idea usually is expressed early in the speech or text.

To render a faithful interpretation, the interpreter must quickly grasp the important parts of the speaker's message and sort out the main ideas from the supporting ideas. This usually happens without benefit of discussion with the speaker. In the speaker's mind and perhaps in the speaker's notes, some points are more important than other points. If the interpreter attributes equal weight to all of the speaker's points, the message may be skewed and certainly will not match the speaker's original message.

Sometimes, the speaker speaks very rapidly or is reading from a prepared speech. When this happens, the interpreter cannot always ask the speaker to pause or repeat information. In those instances, it is even more important for the interpreter to select the most important points. The ideal interpretation includes all the main points and all of the supporting points, in the order originally presented. In real-world practice, this is not always possible. In situations where the interpreter is unable fully keep up with the pace of the speaker's comments, it is necessary for the interpreter to identify main and supporting points. For example, Van Dam (1989) describes a process she calls "hop, skip and jump." By this she means that when the interpreter cannot keep up with the pace of the speaker, the interpreter must "hop" and "skip" over some of the supporting details and "jump" to the next main point. In order to do this, the interpreter must be able to discern which points are central and which are supporting.

During the interpretation process, there is a constant sorting of information. The interpreter must determine which information is very important or less important. Interpreters make this decision based their schema, on what they know about the topic, and what they know about the audience. The interpreter constantly sorts information into categories or topics and decides which points are most important and which are less important.

Analysis of the Target Audience

The interpreter must listen to and comprehend the message with the needs of the target audience in mind. Sometimes interpreters have a clear idea of the composition of the target audience and sometimes they do not. The information about the target audience, even if it is not complete, must be analyzed in order to formulate an interpretation that is relevant to the recipients. The target audience must be analyzed in terms of their composition and information needs. In addition to the actual content and arrangement of the linguistic information, cultural information must be considered. If the interpretation is created without regard to audience needs and cultural context, then the interpretation will not be as accurate or meaningful as it could be.

There are various factors to consider in audience analysis. The first is size. When you interpret for a large group there will be less opportunity for audience interaction with the speaker and with the interpreter. Sometimes this interpreting is done via interpretation equipment for spoken language. In sign language interpreting the interpreter may be standing on stage and not able to see the audience clearly. These types of large group settings limit feedback from the audience to the interpreter during the interpreting process. A smaller audience may allow for more interaction and feedback from the audience to the interpreter. In settings that involve only a few participants there is greater opportunity for feedback to the interpreter. If you are interpreting for a conversation, interview, or dialogue you will have more opportunity to gauge the language styles and preferences of the participants.

In sign language interpreting the interpreter must also be aware that the audience can be heterogeneous in terms of hearing status and signing style preference. The group may consist of only deaf members or some hearing and some deaf. Sometimes the interpreter does not know which participants are deaf or where they are seated in the audience. Another variable that applies to sign language interpreting is the type of signing style that deaf members of the audience prefer. Some deaf people prefer to see signing that strictly follows ASL syntax and others prefer to see signing that follows English syntax. When the audience is a mix of both, the interpreter must use his or her best judgment in selecting a signing style.

The background knowledge of the audience is another important factor in readying yourself to render the interpretation. Sometimes the interpreter is able to get information about the audience's prior knowledge of the subject, but not always. The interpreter may need to make some assumptions about the background knowledge of the target audience. For example, a lecture on Thomas Hopkins Gallaudet, a famous educator of the deaf, is likely to include information relevant to deaf culture. If the audience is deaf, they are likely to have some background knowledge and information on Gallaudet. More generally, at conferences we often assume those in attendance know the jargon and related background information.

It will not always be possible to answer all the questions about the target audience before beginning an interpretation. There may be even more variables than the ones mentioned here. During practice or real interpreting situations, unanswered questions may arise in your mind and the situation may not permit you to clarify. When this happens you must make decisions based on what can be observed, plus what can be inferred from those observations. When working from that position, you must be ready to shift to a different set of assumptions as information builds during the interpreting assignment.

In conclusion, strong comprehension skills form the basis of strong interpreting skills. Main idea identification helps you learn to focus on what is most important and which ideas are supporting. Being able to sort information in this way is valuable for those times during simultaneous interpreting when you are unable to interrupt the speaker or unable to keep up with the speaker's pace. Taking time to analyze the audience and the various participant's needs as best you can in advance of beginning the interpreting assignment provides you with a basis from which to formulate your work. Comprehension has many more facets than those explored in this unit, but these will provide you with some basic approaches to build confidence in your skills.

EXERCISES IN COMPREHENSION

EXERCISE 4.1

Trip to Hong Kong

LESLIE RACH

Directions

This selection is approximately 3 1/2 minutes long. Find a quiet place to work where you will not be interrupted. Answer study question 1. Find the video selection. Adjust the volume as necessary and be sure you can see the TV monitor clearly. Begin by allowing yourself time to focus on the speaker's face. Read the transcript once to familiarize yourself with the topic and then simultaneously interpret the selection. Do not pause or rewind the videotape. Answer the remaining study questions and complete the follow-up.

Study Questions

1. Describe the context and participants for this interpretation based on the exercise title and picture of the speaker.

____

____

2. What is the gist of the passage?

3. What strategies did you use to focus your listening on the speaker's message?

4. What strategies did you use to remember what you heard?

5. Summarize this selection in the space provided.

Transcript for *Trip to Hong Kong,* Leslie Rach

Hi, I'm Leslie Rach and I'm gonna tell a story about a trip I took to Hong Kong four years ago, in the winter. My husband and I were supposed to go from Dulles airport to North Carolina where we would then fly to Tokyo, Japan, and connect on a flight to Hong Kong.

As it turned out we did go to North Carolina and then we spent about five hours in the air and everything was going fine until the pilot made an announcement in Japanese, of course, because we were on Japan airlines. And I should go back and add that when we were on the tarmac in North Carolina, the flight attendants were standing um out by the, where the plane was going to take off and they were waving very formally to wave us goodbye on our way off to Japan. So that was an indication of what was to come.

We uh were about one hour outside of Anchorage Alaska, to the west of Anchorage, and the pilot made an announcement uh, that we would be turning around because of mechanical difficulties and didn't elaborate on that really at all. And everyone seemed unusually calm on the plane. I couldn't believe it. I thought some one should be screaming, although I wasn't screaming, someone should have been. So anyway, he turned the plane around and we ended up landing in a cargo airport in Anchorage, which indicated that it was pretty serious, although none of us really knew it at the time. But as we were landing, on the runway, on either side of where we were landing, there were about 100 ambulances and fire engines lined up all along the runway. And um so then we started to get the feeling that it was pretty serious. And we ended up landing and we got off the plane and went into the airport and through the window we could see that one of the engines, the right engine, was on fire.

And of course none of us had known this the whole time. And several of the passengers immediately got out their cameras and out of the window they started snapping pictures of the burning fuselage. So um it was quite an adventure and we spent the night in an airport in Anchorage, I mean in a hotel in Anchorage that evening. And my husband and I, like I said, thought we were going to Hong Kong, but it was December, and so we were dressed very summer like. I had on a thin wool jacket and very thin summer pants. But we were determined to see some of downtown Anchorage since we were sure it was the only time we would be there in our whole lives. So we did make a little go of the city and there was only about maybe about three hours of daylight even though it was the middle of the day. And it was a very gloomy daylight, I should add.

And the next morning we were to get back on a plane and head for Hong Kong as originally scheduled. And they put us back on the same plane. It was very perplexing. But it turned out they had replaced the engine overnight with another engine that had been flown in from Tokyo. So we all got back on the plane with much trepidation and flew to Hong Kong without event and landed the next day.

So that's the story of my trip, the only trip I took to Asia and I'm supposed to go this winter again. So, I have some reservations, but will be brave.

Five-Step Follow-up

Write at least one positive aspect of your interpretation.

Step 1 **Interpretation Rendered**

Review your entire interpretation. Select the portion that reflects your best work. Transcribe only the portions of the interpretation you would like to improve focusing on errors related to comprehension. You do not need to transcribe the source text. Use the steps outlined below to revise each error that you identify.

Step 2 **Determine Underlying Reason**

Although there are many possible reasons for errors in interpretation, in this analysis you will select one of the following for each error identified in Step 1.

Comprehension

Transfer

Reformulation

Step 3 **Probable Effect of Error on Communicative Function**

After selecting the types of errors, rate each error according to how it impacts the communication, keeping in mind that not all errors are equally serious.

5 = No negative consequences to participants

4 = Consequence of errors is minimal

3 = Consequence of errors is moderate

2 = Consequence of errors is severe

1 = Consequence of errors is grave

Step 4 **Revisions**

Write, and then later record, a revised interpretation for each error that better preserves the meaning of the original source message.

Step 5 **Action Plan for Improvement**

Once you have determined the types of errors and their impact, write down what action you plan to take to improve your work.

EXERCISE 4.2

Installing a New Roof

CHRIS LEWNES

Directions

This selection is approximately 2 minutes long. Find a quiet place to work where you will not be interrupted. Answer study question 1. Find the video selection. Adjust the volume as necessary and be sure you can see the TV monitor clearly. Begin by allowing yourself time to focus on the speaker's face. Read the transcript once and then simultaneously interpret the selection. Do not pause or rewind the videotape. Answer the remaining study questions and complete the follow-up.

Study Questions

1. Describe context and participants for this interpretation based on the exercise title and picture of the speaker.

___

___

2. What is the gist of the passage?

___

___

3. What is the speaker's intent in giving this talk?

___

___

4. What strategies did you use to focus your listening on the speaker's message? What strategies did you use to remember what you heard?

___

___

5. Review your interpretation and look for examples of comments that you made about the interpretation or your performance on the interpretation. Look for examples of extraneous movement, grimacing, or other non-verbal aspects of your work that are likely to be distracting to your audience. Write down the number of times you made comments that were not part of the source message.

Transcript for *Installing a New Roof,* Chris Lewnes

Hello. My name is Chris Lewnes. I'd like to talk about something I've done recently: that's laying a new roof over an existing roof. I'm gonna describe how to lay an asphalt shingle roof over one that is currently in existence. The first what you do is clean the old roof as much as possible. Next, lay a five-foot strip along the base of the old roof. On top of that you're ready to lay your first shingle. The shingles generally are 13 inches wide and 39 inches long. The first row will be 10 inches. Therefore, you have to cut 3 inches from the first row of shingles. After that row, the proceeding rows will be full shingles. In order to get the proper pattern on the roof, you have to go to one edge of the roof and make cuts in the shingles that you first lay. The cuts will be 6 inches, 9 inches, 3 inches, 6 inches, and then a full shingle. Lay the shingles progressively up the roof and the pattern will appear, the same as the old pattern on the roof. Once you get to the top of the roof, or the crown, one should remove the existing crown. Once the shingles are up to the crown, replace that crown using pieces of the shingles. Each shingle is 3 shingles wide—each individual shingle is 13 inches. Cut the shingles so that you have a 13-inch square. Lay the 13-inch squares perpendicular to the roof with a 5-inch overlap. Once this is done your roof is complete, and your new roof should look like the old roof, only brand-new.

Five-Step Follow-up

Write at least one positive aspect of your interpretation.

Step 1

Interpretation Rendered

Review your entire interpretation. Select the portion that reflects your best work. Transcribe only the portions of the interpretation you would like to improve, focusing on errors related to comprehension. You do not need to transcribe the source text. Use the steps outlined below to revise each error that you identify.

Step 2

Determine Underlying Reason

Although there are many possible reasons for errors in interpretation, in this analysis you will select one of the following for each error identified in Step 1.

Comprehension

Transfer

Reformulation

Step 3

Probable Effect of Error on Communicative Function

After selecting the types of errors, rate each error according to how it impacts the communication, keeping in mind that not all errors are equally serious.

5 = No negative consequences to participants

4 = Consequence of errors is minimal

3 = Consequence of errors is moderate

2 = Consequence of errors is severe

1 = Consequence of errors is grave

Step 4 **Revisions**

Write, and then later record, a revised interpretation for each error that better preserves the meaning of the original source message.

____

____

____

Step 5 **Action Plan for Improvement**

Once you have determined the types of errors and their impact, write down what action you plan to take to improve your work.

____

____

EXERCISE 4.3

Encouraging Young Girls

ARLENE FONG CRAIG

Directions

This selection is approximately 5 1/2 minutes long. Find a quiet place to work where you will not be interrupted. Answer study question 1. Find the video selection. Adjust the volume as necessary and be sure you can see the TV monitor clearly. Begin by allowing yourself time to focus on the speaker's face. Read the transcript once and then simultaneously interpret the selection. Do not pause or rewind the videotape. Answer the remaining study questions and complete the follow-up.

Study Questions

1. Describe the context and participants for this interpretation based on the exercise title and picture of the speaker.

____

____

2. What is the gist of the passage?

3. What strategies did you use to focus your listening on the speaker's message?

4. What is the speaker's intent in giving this talk?

5. What does the speaker mean by "outreach programs for free-standing policy research organizations?"

6. What is *The Women of Brewster Place* about?

7. Describe D.C. Girls and state its purpose.

Transcript for *Encouraging Young Girls,* Arlene Fong Craig

Hello. I'm Arlene Fong Craig. I develop and implement education and outreach programs for free-standing policy research organizations. I also manage conferences and publications production.

My current work involves University/Community partnerships—or sometimes, they're called Academic Activist Coalitions. And these are collaborative working relationships between a university or another institution of higher education and community-based organizations.

The program that I'm proudest of—I guess because I had the most fun doing it, and because I think we had the most impact on the community—was D.C. Girls. D.C. Girls is a multicultural arts program for girls who are just reaching adolescence. They're girls that are usually between 10 and 13 years old. We targeted girls, particularly young girls who are African-American or Latina living in metropolitan Washington, D.C. And our purpose was to help the girls learn more about their culture and also about the culture of girls who are their neighbors, but with whom they may not hang out and with whom they may have misunderstandings, or they may have stereotypes of their neighbors.

This program was run by the Union Institute Center for Women. It's a very nontraditional university. It's a university for adult learners. And the Center for Women decided that it would have a program with the community that would really show what the current scholarship is on girls and the university.

I recruited the girls for this program. I stood on church steps, I met with their parents at libraries, and I also visited community-based organizations right on their home turf, and persuaded them it was okay to let go of their babies and to be with us for this one-year program.

We divided D.C. Girls into three sets of workshops: The first one was the tradition of quilts. There's an African-American tradition for quilts, and a Central and South American one. The arpilleras, which are the South American quilts, generally are much more political in nature. And they tell the story, usually, of political oppression in very clear terms. And they were often used as an expression of certain wrongs in the country when people did not have other outlets to express it. African-American quilts generally take a much more wide-ranging form, and they could either be based upon certain repetitive geometric patterns, but more often, they would be, really, left up to the imagination of the creator. So, I recruited a bicultural team of teachers, we had a bicultural classroom full of girls, and they set to work.

The second part of D.C. Girls really focused upon non-print media: media that was music videos, perhaps movies, and television—the kind of media that girls are most likely to get their information from. And what we would do is have a girl select certain music videos that we would discuss and analyze, although we never used that term. And we also selected, ourselves, certain movies we would have the girls watch. And we really tried to encourage a very free discussion about the kinds of images of women and girls that were portrayed in rap videos and in movies. Ironically, a lot of the girls were about 10 years old at this point, and the movie they chose to watch was *The Women of Brewster Place,* which had been produced five years earlier.

And when you think about it, it's not a very current movie by their standards, and it was over half of their lifetime ago, but this is the movie they chose to watch two or three times, and really talk about things that were very central to their lives.

The culminating part of D.C. Girls was their performance at the National Museum for Women in the Arts. And we created a music video, of a sort, of the girls' performance at the museum. We asked the girls, originally, to write a journal of this last portion of D.C. Girls, and we would base their performance upon the journal. But I think some of the issues were too painful for them. So, instead, we decided to adapt a folk tale, *The Girl Who Sat in the Fork of the Tree.* And so, we had the girls make some of the sets. They were minimalist, but they made the tree and they made the doll—again following their own traditions—who sat in the fork of the tree. So, we invited the parents and their families, and we had a wonderful performance at the museum. And afterwards, we had a reception for the girls. And out of this, we produced a 30-minute videotape, and we gave that to each of the girls.

And I think I've discovered what I'd like to do in the next stage of my life: I really enjoyed being executive producer! It was fun, it was a great video, and we provided a service to the community. And that was D.C. Girls!

Five-Step Follow-up

Write at least one positive aspect of your interpretation.

____

Step 1 **Interpretation Rendered**

Review your entire interpretation. Select the 3-minute portion that reflects your best work. Transcribe only the portions of the interpretation you would like to improve. You do not need to transcribe the source text. Use the steps outlined below to revise each error that you identify.

____

Step 2 **Determine Underlying Reason**

Although there are many possible reasons for errors in interpretation, in this analysis you will select one of the following for each error identified in Step 1.

Comprehension

Transfer

Reformulation

Step 3 **Probable Effect of Error on Communicative Function**

After selecting the types of errors, rate each error according to how it impacts the communication, keeping in mind that not all errors are equally serious.

5 = No negative consequences to participants

4 = Consequence of errors is minimal

3 = Consequence of errors is moderate

2 = Consequence of errors is severe

1 = Consequence of errors is grave

Step 4 **Revisions**

Write, and then later record, a revised interpretation for each error that better preserves the meaning of the original source message.

Step 5 Action Plan for Improvement

Once you have determined the types of errors and their impact, write down what action you plan to take to improve your work.

____

____

Progress Tracking Sheet

Use this sheet to track your progress with the exercises you have completed. After performing the exercise (one or two times), answering the study questions, and doing the follow-up, fill in the tracking sheet. Note the date that you completed the exercise and give an indication of your level of accomplishment. You can use either a quantitative or a qualitative approach to track your progress.

Exercise Number	Date	First Performance	Study Questions	Follow-up Activity	Questions and Reminders	Date	Second Performance
Exercise 4.1 Quantitative							
Qualitative							
Exercise 4.2 Quantitative							
Qualitative							
Exercise 4.3 Quantitative							
Qualitative							
Quantitative Totals							

UNIT 5

Transfer

In this unit we briefly explore transfer in simultaneous interpreting and provide a simple and practical approach to managing transfer. Simultaneous interpreting requires that you comprehend and analyze the message, transfer it into the target language mentally, and reformulate the message in the target language. In consecutive interpreting the interpreter can take notes while listening to the source message and refer to the notes to render the interpretation after the source message stops. In simultaneous interpreting note-taking is not possible because the source message is ongoing and so the transfer process relies on the interpreter's cognitive and linguistic skill. In this unit we look at the importance of grasping the relationships between actors and objects and visualizing those relationships as a way to enhance memory of the message, which in turn aids in the transfer process.

Transfer in Simultaneous Interpreting

The transfer process is invisible and does not include the actual rendition of the message. In this phase, the interpreter mentally creates possible interpretations. Because transfer is invisible and cannot be observed directly, we can only make inferences about the transfer process by analyzing the product of the interpretation. If a skewed interpretation is caused by problems in the transfer process it means that the interpreter has enough command of both languages but is not able to accurately convey the message from one language to another. The transfer process is not automatic or intuitive. It requires focused practice. However, during simultaneous interpreting it is difficult to identify discrete aspects of the process since many different cognitive demands are being placed on the interpreter in an ongoing manner.

By developing a simple strategy that is easy to remember and implement, you can improve your transfer skills. First, make some decisions about what the message means or could mean. Gile calls this process developing a *meaning hypothesis*. After you have decided on the meaning or possible meanings of the passage, you can use your visualization skills to help you remember the meaning. A quick way to do this is to map out three types of relationships in your mind: relationships related to time sequencing, relationships between people and objects, and logical relationships. More detail on each of these is presented below.

Meaning Hypothesis

Gile (1995) cautions that interpreting is not really a linear process with well-defined boundaries. Instead, the process may be more like a back-and-forth movement between phases. For example, in the comprehension phase you establish what Gile calls a "meaning hypothesis," in which you temporarily assign a meaning to the part of the text on which you are working. This temporary meaning is based on what you already know about the topic, what you can logically infer, and what you can find out. According to The American Heritage Dictionary (1979, p. 673) infer means "to conclude from evidence." If you do not have enough evidence to make an inference you must leave the interpretation as non-committal as possible until you find out more information. For example, if you are not sure if the gender of the person being referred to is male or female, you need to develop a meaning hypothesis that can be further refined when you know the gender of the person. This distinction may be revealed as the message unfolds. In the interim the interpretation can refer to "a person" or "someone" instead of a man or a woman.

Next you check the meaning hypothesis for plausibility in this context. Gile says that errors can occur if you do not have the background knowledge to fully understand the text. Once you are satisfied that the meaning hypothesis is plausible, you begin to find ways to transfer the message and then move into the reformulation phase. Although this text focuses on one stage at a time, remember that the stages really do not occur in isolation except for purposes of study. Before you can transfer a message you must make some decisions about what the message means using the meaning hypothesis you developed. You may need to revise your hypothesis if new information changes your understanding of the meaning of the source message.

Relationships in the Message

Nida and Tabor (1982) say that during translation there are three types of relations between idea units that you should keep in mind. They are temporal, spatial and logical. Their theories refer to translation and are adapted here to interpreting. During interpreting there is a continuous shifting of attention and cognitive effort. Even so, there are certain relationships that must be kept constant such as the relationships in time sequences and those between people and objects and how these could logically fit together in the context of the message. Awareness of these types of relationships between idea units helps you to analyze and remember the message long enough to interpret it. Keeping these relationships in mind is a simple way to improve the transfer of the message from one language to another. Each of these relationships is summarized below. Keep in mind that it is possible for all three types of relationships to be in operation at the same time. For example, driving directions from point A to point B include a time sequence, relationships among the person, the car, and the starting and ending points and points along the way as well as the logical unfolding of events such as driving without interruption in a forward direction.

Temporal Relationships

Temporal relationships describe the time and sequencing relationships between events. When you are aware of the importance of temporal relationships your analysis of the message can be more precise which allows the transfer process to be more accurate. Nida and Tabor (1982) say temporal relations permit you to include the notion of several events happening at the same time or events that span a long period of time. This aspect of the transfer process becomes especially important when working into languages that structure time-based events differently than the source language. An example of a type of discourse that relies on careful interpretation of temporal events is directions. Driving directions require that the sequence of events be presented in a specific order. Directions for cooking can require that certain ingredients be added before others. In either of these examples, if the temporal order is not preserved, the message will be skewed in the target language.

Spatial Relationships

Spatial relationships allow for two different possibilities. Nida and Tabor (1982) say that "One is between objects such as a house and a tree, and the other is the spatial relationship between the viewer and other objects." Spatial relationships point out the importance of the relationships between the people and objects referred to in the message. For example, in the sentence "She drove past the stop sign," the relationship of the car to the stop sign is important and it changes as the car approaches, is even with the stop sign, and passes it. Spatial relations are especially important in visual languages like American Sign Language. In ASL it is important to establish the identity and location of the people and objects referred to in the space surrounding the signer. The signer must establish whether the objects being referred to are in view and must be consistent in referring to those objects and their relative locations in space.

Visualizing

A valuable tool for developing skill in preserving spatial relationships is visualization. Visualization skills allow you to see in your mind's eye where people are in relation to each other, where people are in relation to objects, and objects' relationships to each other. For example, a text may refer to a person speaking to a woman and giving her a pen. The text may not reveal which person is to the right and which is to the left or if they are facing each other. If you are working into a visual language, you must establish the people and objects in locations in space and then refer back to them systematically and consistently.

Schweda Nicholson (1996) says that the visuospatial sketch pad is a construct that can assist in developing memory and accuracy in interpretation. To do this, the interpreter must hear the incoming message or source language and perform various mental manipulations to free the message from its original form. One way to do this is to create a visual image.

It is sometimes crucial to know the actual location of objects or persons in relation to each other, and at other times it is sufficient to know simply that things are in relation to each other. If you do not know the actual location of the objects or people, you must create a visualization and use it as a point of reference until the actors or objects shift location. Use hypothesis testing to establish locations until you find evidence of actual locations.

If you sense that the exact relationship is important, then you may need to ask the speaker for clarification. Examples of instances where this kind of information is essential could include situations where directions are being given to create something, such as in a recipe or a building plan. Another instance where it is important to know the actual relationship is legal testimony, where the exact relationship and location of persons and objects can be very important.

Logical Relationships

Logical relations are the third type of relationship between idea units that Nida and Tabor (1982) discuss. Logical relations refer to "cause and effect or condition and consequence." Languages may differ in how they arrange cause-and-effect clauses such as the if-then clause in English. Experiences within the cultures that you interpret between will also come into play in considering logical relations. For example, if the source message indicates that the doorbell rang and someone answered the door, it is logical to assume that a person walked to the door and opened it, even though the act of walking was not explicitly stated. The condition of the door bell ringing causes the consequence of someone walking to the door.

Being aware of the importance of these types of relationships can help reduce the cognitive load during interpretation. For example, the more automatic it becomes to rely on visualization to help remember the location of objects and people in relation to each other and how these things interact over time, the more cognitive capacity you will have for processing information.

The material in this unit encourages you hypothesize about meaning and visualize situations. Your mind constantly creates hypotheses about what the speaker means and about what the speaker might say. While the creation of hypotheses is important, it is also important to realize that not all hypotheses will actually be borne out. It is the mark of a skilled interpreter to realize that there may be more than one possible hypothesis and that one or more may need to be discarded in order to convey the meaning intended by the speaker.

As you work through the exercises in this unit, consciously develop a meaning hypothesis, keeping it non-committal if necessary, and then visualize time sequences, relationships between people and objects, and the logical flow of events.

In summary, the types of relationships to keep in mind as you simultaneously interpret are temporal, spatial, and logical. Temporal relationships describe the time and sequencing relationships between events. Logical relations refer to "cause and effect or condition and consequence" (Nida and Tabor, 1982). Spatial relationships point out the importance of the relationships between the people and objects referred to in the message.

EXERCISES IN TRANSFER

EXERCISE 5.1

The Payroll Process

JEFF HARDISON

Directions

This selection is approximately 3 minutes long. Find a quiet place to work where you will not be interrupted. Answer study question 1. Find the video selection. Adjust the volume as necessary and be sure you can see the TV monitor clearly. Begin by allowing yourself time to focus on the speaker's face. Record yourself simultaneously interpreting the selection. Notice the hypotheses you develop and that you mentally "try out" interpretations before rendering an interpretation. Visualize relationships between events, people and objects, and the logical flow of events. Do not pause or rewind the source tape. Answer the remaining study questions and complete the follow-up.

Study Questions

1. Describe context and participants for this interpretation based on the exercise title and picture of the speaker.

____

____

2. Find an example of spatial relationships. Are these relationships preserved in your interpretation?

3. Find an example of temporal relations. Are these relations preserved in your interpretation?

4. What are the logical relations in this text? Does your interpretation preserve the message and the logical relations?

5. Write one hypothesis that you developed that proved to be accurate. Write one hypothesis that you developed that proved to be inaccurate.

Transcript for *The Payroll Process*, Jeff Hardison

Hello. My name is Jeff Hardison. You know, in corporate America today, probably the largest single expense that any business has is its payroll. So, I thought that it might be interesting to kinda talk a little bit about how timecards actually get translated and become checks—that process, and how that happens. It's actually less complicated than I thought. I had a friend of mine, who is a CPA, kinda go through the process for me.

What usually happens in the beginning is that you have an individual who will fill out a timecard. And then that timecard has to be taken to be approved by somebody who has the authority to do so, typically the supervisor of whatever corporation, or business, or unit that we're talking about.

After that, then, the timecard gets submitted into the accounting department. Now, what the accounting department does, at this point, is they take the card, and then they pull up what they have on the computer, typically, nowadays, they use computers. They will pull up a log of all of the employees that work there and match up numbers, to ensure that, in fact, the employee is an existing employee, active, because this is one of the first checks that are used in order to prevent someone from trying to embezzle or illegally get money out of a company that they ought not to.

Once that's been done, then what happens is that they then input the number of hours that the individual has had into what they call an "automated payroll system." So they pull up specifically a kind of program, a computer program that you then feed in that employee's number with the hours. What's really nice about the computer programs is that it will automatically do all of the tax work for you. It will do the Federal tax, it will do the State tax, it will take care of annual leave, sick leave; it will divide all of that up. Also, if you have situations where, perhaps, a corporation does different jobs, it will begin to actually compartmentalize which jobs were done by that individual. The reason that's so much nicer now in computers is that in the days before computers that actually all had to be figured by hand. You can imagine how much time that would have taken for someone to have to do manually.

Once that's been done, then you're basically pretty much ready to go and start printing the checks. What you then do, once the information, as I said, has been input, is you then go through and do what's called a "first edit." What that is, is that you go back and check to ensure that the information that you've inputted actually matches what is supposed to be there, so that you haven't done something in error. Then, you go to the printer, if that's where you do it. Some corporations, now, do not actually print their checks in their own place of business. They'll often have another corporation or other business handle that, but for those that do, you would then go to the printer, and then you would put your checks in, feed it into the printer, and then basically hit "print." Then, all of the checks come through. Then, they go through what's called the "second edit," which is basically physically looking at the checks. Now, that depends, again, on the size of your corporation—if it's really huge, and you're talking, you know, several hundreds or even thousands of people, obviously that's not practical. But, if it's a smaller corporation or business, and you can actually do that, you'll do what's called a "second check." Or, just ensure that every check that's been printed was in fact a check that needed to be, or matches up to what all of the employees have done. After that, someone is usually delegated to tear them apart, put them into an envelope, it's distributed to everybody, and happy hour hits, and everyone's happy.

Five-Step Follow-up

Write at least one positive aspect of your interpretation.

Step 1 Interpretation Rendered

Review your entire interpretation. Select the portion that reflects your best work. Transcribe only the portions of the interpretation you would like to improve. You do not need to transcribe the source text. Use the steps outlined below to revise each error that you identify.

Step 2 **Determine Underlying Reason**

Although there are many possible reasons for errors in interpretation, in this analysis you will select one of the following for each error identified in Step 1.

Comprehension

Transfer

Reformulation

Step 3 **Probable Effect of Error on Communicative Function**

After selecting the types of errors, rate each error according to how it impacts the communication, keeping in mind that not all errors are equally serious.

5 = No negative consequences to participants

4 = Consequence of errors is minimal

3 = Consequence of errors is moderate

2 = Consequence of errors is severe

1 = Consequence of errors is grave

Step 4 **Revisions**

Write, and then later record, a revised interpretation for each error that better preserves the meaning of the original source message.

Step 5 Action Plan for Improvement

Once you have determined the types of errors and their impact, write down what action you plan to take to improve your work.

____

____

____

EXERCISE 5.2

Driving from San Diego to Tucson

AMBER LEWNES

Directions

This selection is approximately 1 1/2 minutes long. Find a quiet place to work where you will not be interrupted. Answer study question 1. Find the video selection. Adjust the volume as necessary and be sure you can see the TV monitor clearly. Begin by allowing yourself time to focus on the speaker's face. Record yourself simultaneously interpreting the selection. Notice the hypotheses you develop and that you mentally "try out" interpretations before rendering an interpretation. Visualize relationships between events, people and objects, and the logical flow of events. Do not pause or rewind the source tape. Answer the remaining study questions and complete the follow-up.

Study Questions

1. Describe context and participants for this interpretation based on the exercise title and the picture of the speaker.

   ____

   ____

   ____

2. Find an example of spatial relationships. Are these relationships preserved in your interpretation?

3. Find an example of temporal relations. Are these relations preserved in your interpretation?

4. What are the logical relations in this text? Does your interpretation preserve the message and the logical relations?

5. Write one hypothesis that you developed that proved to be accurate. Write one hypothesis that you developed that proved to be inaccurate.

Transcript for *Driving from San Diego to Tucson,* Amber Lewnes

My name is Amber Lewnes and I'm gonna give you directions on how to get from San Diego, California, to Tucson, Arizona.

The first thing you do is you get on the freeway 15 South and keep going until you find the 8, and go 8 East and you'll follow that all the way through the desert and you'll pass some sand dunes and the Arizona border and a sign that tells you whether or not you want to go to Phoenix or Tucson. And then you take the 10 West to Tucson, and you follow that until you get to a road called Speedway. And this is how you get to the campus of University of Arizona, which is where I used to go quite often on my trips back and forth to school. You take a right onto Speedway and you follow that road down until you see the campus. And if you take a left onto Campbell you'll get to go through the entrance of the campus. Then you make a right onto the campus itself and you can follow that down where you'll see the gym and the library and the sports arena that they have. There's all sorts of lawns and art sculptures that you can follow along to look and see more of the campus. And that's University of Arizona. That's it.

Five-Step Follow-up

Write at least one positive aspect of your interpretation.

Step 1 **Interpretation Rendered**

Review your entire interpretation. Select the portion that reflects your best work. Transcribe only the portions of the interpretation you would like to improve. You do not need to transcribe the source text. Use the steps outlined below to revise each error that you identify.

Step 2 **Determine Underlying Reason**

Although there are many possible reasons for errors in interpretation, in this analysis you will select one of the following for each error identified in Step 1.

Comprehension

Transfer

Reformulation

____

____

Step 3 **Probable Effect of Error on Communicative Function**

After selecting the types of errors, rate each error according to how it impacts the communication, keeping in mind that not all errors are equally serious.

5 = No negative consequences to participants

4 = Consequence of errors is minimal

3 = Consequence of errors is moderate

2 = Consequence of errors is severe

1 = Consequence of errors is grave

____

____

Step 4 **Revisions**

Write, and then later record, a revised interpretation for each error that better preserves the meaning of the original source message.

____

____

____

Step 5 **Action Plan for Improvement**

Once you have determined the types of errors and their impact, write down what action you plan to take to improve your work.

____

____

____

EXERCISE 5.3

Courage

PETER LEARY

Directions

This selection is approximately 7 1/2 minutes long. Find a quiet place to work where you will not be interrupted. Answer study question 1. Find the video selection. Adjust the volume as necessary and be sure you can see the TV monitor clearly. Begin by allowing yourself time to focus on the speaker's face. Your teacher may require you to study or translate this passage in advance of interpreting it. Record yourself simultaneously interpreting the selection. Notice the hypotheses you develop and that you mentally "try out" interpretations before rendering an interpretation. Visualize relationships between events, people and objects, and the logical flow of events. Do not pause or rewind the source tape. Answer the remaining study questions and complete the follow-up.

Study Questions

1. Describe the context and participants for this interpretation based on the exercise title and picture of the speaker.

____

____

2. Find an example of spatial relationships. Are these relationships preserved in your interpretation?

____

____

3. Find an example of temporal relations. Are these relations preserved in your interpretation?

____

____

____

4. What are the logical relations in this text? Does your interpretation preserve the message and the logical relations?

5. Write one hypothesis that you developed that proved to be accurate. Write one hypothesis that you developed that proved to be inaccurate.

Transcript for *Courage*, Peter Leary

Hello. I'm Peter Leary. I'm here to talk about courage. Courage. Courage is a virtue, and by its very nature does not fall within the bounds of any set definition.

The concept of courage has been explained by so many philosophers, soldiers, and ditch diggers that their views could fill a plethora of books. Webster's dictionary defines courage as "the state or quality of mind or spirit that enables one to face danger and overcome fear." This suitably vague definition is roughly the guideline that most people will attribute to this virtue; however, it can also be fleshed out by the words of a number of philosophers.

Aristotle is one of the greatest and well-known of these philosophers. In his book *Nicomachean Ethics,* spelled N-I-C-O-M-A-C-H-E-A-N, he talked in great lengths about courage and fear. And he defined courage as "any act that overcomes fear." Thus, by this definition, I feel this man, though he defied death, still would not be courageous; where a boy who conquered their fear of the dark would be courageous. Another facet of Aristotle's definition was that all courage was equal. The same boy who conquered his fear of the dark was equally courageous with a besieged military commander against insurmountable odds. The last attribute of Aristotle's courage was that it was like a muscle: the more you used it, the better it got. The more courageous you were, the easier acts of courage became. Another view of courage is embodied in the phrase "Angels rush in—fools rush in where angels fear to tread." This view holds that there is a point at which courage becomes foolishness or lunacy. It takes Aristotle's definition and puts boundaries around it. Instead of "any act of overcoming fear" it is "any act of overcoming fear within reason." Adherents to this view might use the example of a family defending their house: were they to throw out two or three thieves in the night that would be courageous. But to defy an army who threatened to burn their house—that would be lunacy.

Both of these views have used an act—the act of overcoming fear—as their defining point. Thus, by looking at courageous actions you can learn more about courage. And one thing you learn is that courage is contagious. Take for instance Mahatma Gandhi. He was a lawyer who professed a fear of authority. Yet he overcame that fear and inspired a nation to revolt—to throw off British rule and to govern themselves. His courage inspired thousands. Another example is of the Spartan warrior Leonides. When told that the army of Xerxes was coming to invade his land, he volunteered to stand alone in a narrow pass to hold the army at bay so that the cities beyond the pass would have time to fortify their defenses. His courage inspired 300 more warriors to stand with him, and they held off the army for a day, their own 300 wounding 10,000 of the opposing army and giving their citizens time to prepare their defenses. Both of these examples lend credence to something that people say every day: If you do it, I'll do it. If you are courageous, I will use your inspiration to make me courageous.

Another thing that can be gleaned from looking at these acts are that courage is viewed through value systems. Were a man to defy his fear of hell and murder 10,000 children he would not be courageous. Yet not all of these examples are as black and white; most are gray. Is it courageous to support abortion, or pro-life? Courage is in the eyes of the beholder.

In conclusion, although the thoughts of mankind are widely arrayed on the concept of courage; even though one man's courage is another man's foolishness; even though all acts of courage may not be equal—there are unifying aspects which run through most views of courage. These common aspects are very similar to Webster's definition, with a few minor changes. Taking into account both the lives and words of men and women throughout history, a better definition might read: Courage is a virtue that exemplifies an individual's triumph over fear in order to do something righteous and rational.

Five-Step Follow-up

Write at least one positive aspect of your interpretation.

Step 1 Interpretation Rendered

Review your entire interpretation. Select the 3-minute portion that reflects your best work. Transcribe only the portions of the interpretation you would like to improve. You do not need to transcribe the source text. Use the steps outlined below to revise each error that you identify.

Step 2 Determine Underlying Reason

Although there are many possible reasons for errors in interpretation, in this analysis you will select one of the following for each error identified in Step 1.

Comprehension

Transfer

Reformulation

____

____

Step 3 **Probable Effect of Error on Communicative Function**

After selecting the types of errors, rate each error according to how it impacts the communication, keeping in mind that not all errors are equally serious.

5 = No negative consequences to participants

4 = Consequence of errors is minimal

3 = Consequence of errors is moderate

2 = Consequence of errors is severe

1 = Consequence of errors is grave

____

____

Step 4 **Revisions**

Write, and then later record, a revised interpretation for each error that better preserves the meaning of the original source message.

____

____

____

____

Step 5 **Action Plan for Improvement**

Once you have determined the types of errors and their impact, write down what action you plan to take to improve your work.

____

____

____

Progress Tracking Sheet

Use this sheet to track your progress with the exercises you have completed. After performing the exercise (one or two times), answering the study questions, and doing the follow-up, fill in the tracking sheet. Note the date that you completed the exercise and give an indication of your level of accomplishment. You can use either a quantitative or a qualitative approach to track your progress.

Exercise Number	Date	First Performance	Study Questions	Follow-up Activity	Questions and Reminders	Date	Second Performance
Exercise 5.1 Quantitative							
Qualitative							
Exercise 5.2 Quantitative							
Qualitative							
Exercise 5.3 Quantitative							
Qualitative							
Quantitative Totals							

UNIT 6

Reformulation

Reformulation is the visible or audible result of the interpretation process. Reformulation allows the message to take form in the target language. Reformulation is the third part of the three-part paradigm for the interpreting process that we are using in this text, keeping in mind that interpreting is really a complex, dynamic, multilevel cognitive operation. The message must be expressed in word choices that are appropriate to the target language, conform to the target language syntax, and preserve the illocutionary force of the source text. This stage of the interpreting process allows you to focus on creating a product as the result of the processes you have used so far.

Reformulation depends on the source message for a variety of reasons. Gile (1995) explains that individuals tend to have verbal habits, but that while interpreting these usual approaches to expression are superceded by the fact that the "interpreter must follow the path of the source language speaker" (p.166). Gile goes on to say that sometimes the interpreter can pattern the interpretation on lexical choices in the source language, but this approach can be risky as it may lead to a transcoding rather than a faithful interpretation. The following sections deal with specific aspects of reformulation in simultaneous interpretation and specific skills that play a role in reformulating the message.

Find the Gist

Being able to state the gist or overall idea of the message in a concise manner is a way to help you begin to correctly reformulate the message in the target language. The speaker may state the topic and provide information that supports the stated topic. At other times the speaker may state a topic and not address it. Sometimes the speaker does not state the topic and you may need to infer the topic in order to understand the text as a whole. Remember that inferring is not guessing. Regardless of whether the speaker states the topic, you must still have an overall idea of what the message is about, whether you are dealing with a sentence or a passage.

Reformulate the Location of Actors and Objects

As part of the reformulation process you need to establish a location for each of the actors and objects. Once you have a mental picture in mind you need to carefully consider how you will correctly render the location of the actors and objects in relation to each other. During the transfer process you asked yourself some questions to help organize the information in your mind. Who or what is doing the acting or initiating the action? Who or what is receiving the action? What is the action? What is the reaction? Sometimes this information is explicit and easy to find in the source message and sometimes it is not. In either case you need to be aware of the locations and the possible locations of actors and objects.

Reformulate Specific Concepts and Relationships

Visualizing the location of actors and objects is necessary before assigning a mental location to each of the actors and objects in relation to each other. Assigning a physical location to actors is necessary in signed languages. Spoken language interpreters may or may not need to explicitly state the relationships between objects or actors, but it is helpful to have a mental image of what is occurring in the message. Be sure to visualize before you begin reformulating the message and keep the same mental image so your interpretation will be consistent.

Reformulate Illocutionary Force

The arrangement of information at the grammatical level of the source text lets us know whether the text is a statement, question, rhetorical question, or exclamation. These various types of utterances have specific functions or illocutionary force. The interpretation must reflect the same discourse function as the source message. For example, if the source text is a question and you convey it as a statement, the function of the statement is not held constant and the effect of the interpretation will be different from that of the source text. You must know how to construct the appropriate syntactic arrangement in the target language in order to create an equivalent impact on the target language audience.

Reformulation at the Word Level

Once you have considered the overall meaning of the source message, you can begin to develop specific word selection techniques. Some source language words will have equivalent lexical items in the target language. In those instances, it will be relatively easy to select the appropriate target language word. This does not mean that you can always use a word replacement technique. You must keep the intent and context of the overall message in mind while you interpret. Bell (1991) wrote about translation methods and suggested several methods of choosing lexical equivalents that can also apply to interpretation.

One method of choosing lexical equivalents is *borrowing*. This means using or borrowing a word directly from the source text and using it in the target text. For example, the word "computer" is used in French, even though it is an English word. The word "computer" will be recognizable in spoken French as the word "computer." This method has application if the source and target language are both spoken or if both languages are signed.

A second method of choosing lexical equivalents is *modulation*. This represents a shift in the point of view—the difference between asking "is this seat taken?" and "is this seat free?" Another example is seen in the fact that "no vacancy" and "full" convey the same concept from opposite viewpoints. The source can convey one point of view while the interpretation conveys a different point of view. It is important that the change in point of view does not change the meaning.

A third method is *adaptation*. This means selecting a culturally equivalent target language response. Bell suggests that in French people say "*bon apetit*" before eating a meal, but in English the equivalent may be silence (p. 71). Speakers of American English may say nothing or may say something like "dig in" or "let's eat" at the beginning of a meal.

Bell explains that when a word or concept has more than one possible translation, you automatically eliminate one possibility in favor of another. Suppose that the source language has only one way to express "joy" while the target language has a variety of ways to express the concept of joy. You must select one from the range of possible choices in the target language. The word that you select has a slightly different meaning from the ones that you reject. This is the point at which the risk of error plays a role in interpretation. He reminds us that it is important to be aware of all of the possible choices in the target language and to know the ramifications of selecting one word over other choices. This linguistic flexibility is only possible when you have strong language skills.

The reformulation process naturally includes the possibility of some loss of meaning in the target language. Some loss is inevitable in interpretation due to the differences in cultures and the limitations of one language to fully convey the cultural constructs of another language. Ideally, linguistic and cultural competence in the two languages you are using, along with clear reasons for the choices you make while interpreting, can minimize loss. As you work through the exercises in this unit focus on the importance of reformulation in interpreting.

EXERCISES IN REFORMULATION

EXERCISE 6.1

The Criminal Justice System

EUGENE CORBETT

Directions

This selection is approximately 4 1/2 minutes long. Find a quiet place to work where you will not be interrupted. Answer study question 1. Find the video selection. Adjust the volume as necessary and be sure you can see the TV monitor clearly. Begin by allowing yourself time to focus on the speaker's face. Record yourself simultaneously interpreting the selection. Pay close attention to your reformulation strategies. Do not pause or rewind the source tape. Answer the remaining study questions and complete the follow-up.

Study Questions

1. Describe the context and participants for this interpretation based on the exercise title and picture of the speaker.

   ____

   ____

2. What is the gist of the selection?

   ____

   ____

   ____

3. Review your interpretation and compare it to the source text to determine whether the location of actors and objects has been appropriately reformulated in the target language.

   ____

   ____

4. Review your interpretation and compare it to the source text to determine whether concepts and relationships between concepts have been appropriately reformulated in the target language.

5. Does your interpretation maintain the illocutionary force of the original?

Transcript for *The Criminal Justice System,* Eugene Corbett

Today I'd like to give you an overview of the criminal justice system in America. The systems ranged throughout the country are somewhat different but all achieve the same purpose. There are basically four parts of the criminal justice system: the arrest phase, the prosecution phase, the arraignment phase in court, and the correctional aspect. These components all to—go together to make up the criminal justice system. They—as I said earlier, they vary depending on the county, the state and also the federal level. As you know, there are various arresting agencies in this country: the FBI, Secret Service, as well as the metropolitan police department.

Let's start with phase one. A person—when a person is arrested, there's probable cause to believe that he or she has committed a crime. At that point, the police officer will escort the individual under arrest for processing. There are several things that happen during the processing stage. The person is booked, as they say sometimes. And during that process the police officer will run a criminal record check to see whether the person has any other charges or is wanted by other state or county officials. He or she is also fingerprinted and that information is sent to the FBI.

Subsequently to that, the individual is brought before the court. That is called the initial appearance. At that time the prosecutor will determine whether or not there is probable cause to believe that this individual has committed an offense. There is also the point that if there's no probable cause to believe the person can be released, and this is called "no paper." The case is then "no-papered." If the prosecutor feels that the individual has committed offense, he will hold the case for what is called a preliminary hearing. At this point the defendant appears before the court for what is called, again, the preliminary hearing. It is at that time the prosecutor will present evidence before the judge as to the defendant's conduct in the community, for that particular crime. If the court finds probable cause at that point, the individual will be detained for a arraignment. It is also during that time that the charges can be lessened from, for example, assault to simple assault. And also the defendant may be able to play—play—plead guilty to a lesser included offense such as simple assault. If not, the case continues to the arraignment part.

The arraignment part will consider the defendant appearing before the court, at which time he or she will plead guilty or not guilty to the formal charges presented by the prosecutor. The formal charges are made up of two forms: one is called an indictment, the other called an information. The information is the formal charges, written charges by the prosecutor. The indictment is handed down from the grand jury. At this time, the defendant, if he pleads guilty to the offense is—a trial date is set. During trial, if the defendant is found guilty he is then sent to the probation office on preparation for a pre-sentence report, and sentencing is set. At that time, the defendant is found—is sentenced and he's incarcerated at the criminal justice system part. He will remain in custody of the department of corrections or whatever correctional facility for the time he is sentenced and released on parole.

Five-Step Follow-up

Write at least one positive aspect of your interpretation.

Step 1 **Interpretation Rendered**

Review your entire interpretation. Select the 3-minute portion that reflects your best work. Transcribe only the portions of the interpretation you would like to improve, focusing on reformulation errors. You do not need to transcribe the source text. Use the steps outlined below to revise each error that you identify.

Step 2 **Determine Underlying Reason**

Although there are many possible reasons for errors in interpretation, in this analysis you will select one of the following for each error identified in Step 1.

Comprehension

Transfer

Reformulation

Step 3 **Probable Effect of Error on Communicative Function**

After selecting the types of errors, rate each error according to how it impacts the communication, keeping in mind that not all errors are equally serious.

5 = No negative consequences to participants

4 = Consequence of errors is minimal

3 = Consequence of errors is moderate

2 = Consequence of errors is severe

1 = Consequence of errors is grave

____

____

Step 4 **Revisions**

Write, and then later record, a revised interpretation for each error that better preserves the meaning of the original source message.

____

____

____

____

Step 5 **Action Plan for Improvement**

Once you have determined the types of errors and their impact, write down what action you plan to take to improve your work.

____

____

EXERCISE 6.2

How to Put in a Zipper

MARQUESSA BROWN

Directions

This selection is approximately 6 minutes long. This selection appeared in *Cognitive Processing in English* in the unit on delayed repetition and may be familiar to you. Find a quiet place to work where you will not be interrupted. Answer study question 1. Find the video selection. Adjust the volume as necessary and be sure you can see the TV monitor clearly. Begin by allowing yourself time to focus on the speaker's face. Record yourself simultaneously interpreting the selection. Pay close attention to your reformulation strategies. Do not pause or rewind the source tape. Answer the remaining study questions and complete the follow-up.

Study Questions

1. Describe the context and participants for this interpretation based on the exercise title and picture of the speaker.

   ____

   ____

   ____

2. What is the gist of the selection?

   ____

   ____

   ____

3. Review your interpretation and compare it to the source text to determine whether the location of actors and objects has been appropriately reformulated in the target language.

   ____

   ____

4. Review your interpretation and compare it to the source text to determine whether concepts and relationships between concepts have been appropriately reformulated in the target language.

   ____

   ____

5. Does your interpretation maintain the illocutionary force of the original?

   ____

   ____

Transcript for *How to Put in a Zippper,* Marquessa Brown

Hi. My name is Marquessa Brown. I'm going to share with you some very simple instructions for putting a zipper in a dress. I believe I'll start with the assumption that everybody listening to this or looking at this isn't going to know two things: they're not going to know how to use a sewing machine, and they're not going to know how to sew. So let me start with some very simple directions about a sewing machine and how you operate it. A sewing machine has a big wheel on the right. It has a needle and um, a needle foot in the center. And it has a plate on the bottom. The plate that's on the bottom is directly over the needle, which is located in the needle foot. It also has a pedal that's on the floor. Now the object is, you have to mash the pedal with your right foot while holding the fabric with two hands so that the fabric can easily glide through the needle. And you've gotta hold it to kinda keep it from going in all kinds of directions so that your fabric won't be crooked and lines everywhere and it's sewn incorrectly. So you're going to—you don't have to worry too much about the wheel. The wheel just turns automatically. But you've gotta learn how to get the right amount of pressure on the foot—on the foot as you're guiding the fabric through. OK, so that's pretty much how the machine works.

Now, there are two ways that you can put a zipper in. You can put the zipper into your garment before you've sewn the entire garment together, or you can complete the entire garment and then put your zipper in. I think it's probably easier to put the zipper in before you've sewn the entire garment together, because you just have less fabric to work with, and I think that makes it a little bit easier when you're trying to guide the fabric through the machine and over the needle. OK.

Now I'm just gonna talk very quickly about how you do it either way. If you want to put the zipper in before you've put your entire garment together, then you want to start with the pieces that the zipper is going to fit in. So let's assume that we're making a skirt, and we're going to have the zipper in the back of the skirt. The zi—the skirt therefore is going to have an opening in the center and the zipper is going to fit directly in this center opening. So what you're going to do—and I think for new sewers it's probably best to do what we call a basting first. A basting basically means that you sew your zipper in by hand first; simply using a needle and thread just sew it up one side and you sew it up the other side. It's very important to make sure that the fabric totally covers the zipper. So often when people are—are learning to sew and putting in zippers for the first time, they tend to have the silver or the shiny part of the zipper showing in the middle. But the key when you're basting is to be sure that the left and the right cover the center of the zipper when you baste it in. OK, so let's say you've sewn up the left side, you've sewn up the right side, the zipper has—the fabric is totally covering the zipper so that you cannot see your zipper. Now, after you've done that and you've got this one piece of fabric: the back part of your dress. You're going to take it and you're going to lift up the needle. There's a little flipper on the back of your sewing machine. So you flip it up, you take your fabric, you put it under there. It's probably better to start sewing on the right side of your zipper.

So, you take your fabric, you put it under, you let down the lever, you put your foot on the pedal and you start sewing. Guiding your fabric all the time. And you want to slow—and you want to sew very slowly. So you're gonna start probably at the bottom and you're gonna sew up one side. Now, if you know anything about zippers the top part of the zipper's kinda thick. So it's going to be important when you're sewing that when you get to the top part and the needle doesn't go over the thick part of the zipper that you stop at that point. So you're gonna sew straight up until you get to that thick part of the zipper and you can't sew it any more. You stop, take the—this is when you're gonna use your wheel on the side. You take your wheel and you turn it up so that the needle comes out of your material. You take your fabric out—um—and then you move it over to the other side. So you're gonna sew again where you did your basting, and you're gonna sew that up. When you finish with that, you take it out again, you pull your zipper down, and then you're gonna sew those two places on both sides where it was too thick to sew it with the—um—zipper up. So now that you've got the zipper pulled down you can get your needle to go through on both sides. That's basically how you put a zipper in.

Five-Step Follow-up

Write at least one positive aspect of your interpretation.

____

Step 1 **Interpretation Rendered**

Review your entire interpretation. Select the 3-minute portion that reflects your best work. Transcribe only the portions of the interpretation you would like to improve, focusing on reformulation errors. You do not need to transcribe the source text. Use the steps outlined below to revise each error that you identify.

____

____

____

Step 2 **Determine Underlying Reason**

Although there are many possible reasons for errors in interpretation, in this analysis you will select one of the following for each error identified in Step 1.

Comprehension

Transfer

Reformulation

____

Step 3

Probable Effect of Error on Communicative Function

After selecting the types of errors, rate each error according to how it impacts the communication, keeping in mind that not all errors are equally serious.

5 = No negative consequences to participants

4 = Consequence of errors is minimal

3 = Consequence of errors is moderate

2 = Consequence of errors is severe

1 = Consequence of errors is grave

Step 4

Revisions

Write, and then later record, a revised interpretation for each error that better preserves the meaning of the original source message.

Step 5

Action Plan for Improvement

Once you have determined the types of errors and their impact, write down what action you plan to take to improve your work.

EXERCISE 6.3

Bulbs for Your Garden

DAVID BURNIGHT

Directions

This selection is approximately 8 minutes long. Find a quiet place to work where you will not be interrupted. Answer study question 1. Find the video selection. Adjust the volume as necessary and be sure you can see the TV monitor clearly. Begin by allowing yourself time to focus on the speaker's face. Record yourself simultaneously interpreting the selection. Pay close attention to your reformulation strategies. Do not pause or rewind the source tape. Answer the remaining study questions and complete the follow-up.

Study Questions

1. Describe the context and participants for this exercise based on the exercise title and picture of the speaker.

____

____

____

2. What is the gist of the selection?

____

____

____

3. Review your interpretation and compare it to the source text to determine whether the location of actors and objects has been appropriately reformulated in the target language.

____

____

____

4. Review your interpretation and compare it to the source text to determine whether concepts and relationships between concepts have been appropriately reformulated in the target language.

5. Does your interpretation maintain the illocutionary force of the original?

Transcript for *Bulbs for Your Garden,* David Burnight

Hello. My name is David Burnight. Let's talk about planting bulbs in your garden. Bulbs are the easiest and least worrisome thing that you can do to have a beautiful garden without anxiety. Give them a little water and they'll come up almost anywhere they're planted, in sun or in shade. Uh, some will even come up between cracks in the pavement; and they will grow in little rock gardens.

Uh, there's almost nothing you can do (except put too much water on them) to keep a bulb from growing. And if you choose varieties carefully you can have blooms in the early spring all the way through to summer, and you'll have lots of colors. Strictly speaking, daffodils, narcissus, tulips, lilies, and hyacinths are the main flowers which a botanist would say actually grow from bulbs. And onions and garlic—they also have flowers. If you cut a bulb in half you'll see that it has layers which are leaves getting ready to sprout, and inside is a tiny bud ready to come up.

There are other flowers which grow from lumps which you plant in the ground—one group comes from what is called a—a corm, a fibrous kind of thing; uh, Dutch iris and um, crocus are examples of this. And then there are tubers, which is a starchy underground storage place for energy which has eyes which become little sprouts. A potato is a tuber, but uh, anemones are a beautiful garden flowers which grow from tubers. All of these can be planted in the same way as bulbs.

My very favorites are daffodils and narcissus because they're so easy. They uh, uh, they're hardy and gophers don't like to eat them. Now tulips are something else. Uh, a gopher considers a tulip bulb a great delicacy and will go quite a distance to eat one, so if you have gophers in your garden give up on tulips unless you're prepared to plant them in little wire baskets under the earth. But gophers do not like dand—uh, daffodil bulbs and they will avoid them; in fact, some gardeners put daffodil bulbs in between other plants to scare the gophers away.

Planting time for bulbs is in the fall to get ready for spring blooming. You'll go to the nursery to buy new bulbs and the best time to buy them is in September when they first come on the market and you have the best choice, but then you need to put them in a cool place—a cool, dry place to store them until planting time. Uh, it's not necessary to cool daffodils very much, but uh, hyacinths and tulips and crocus almost have to be cooled in a refrigerator from 40 to 50 degrees for at least six weeks. This is because they are uh, natives of cold climates and, where in their native country they were chilled underground and they like the cold to convince them that it's time to wake up in the spring.

Here in southern California we plant our bulbs, uh, in November or December just before the winter rains come, and in other climates they need to be planted just before frost time. Now, to choose a spot in the garden, uh, where you have some space and where there is, uh, good soil. The soil needs to be light enough to let water through. If you have hard, clay-like soil it's best to work in some organic material like sawdust or composted leaves or old manure. Um, in my case I have a neighbor who keeps horses and he piles the manure outside the fence and makes it available to anybody who wants it. Now of course, fresh manure would burn bulbs or flowers, but after it's aged a while and, uh, gotten dry it's almost like straw. And it's very easy to scatter several inches of manure on the soil and then just dig it in.

The bulbs need to be buried with the point up and they need to be covered with four to six inches of soil. The ideal depth varies with the species or the variety, but in general, uh, you need to put about twice as much soil on top of 'em as the height of the bulb itself; that is, if a bulb is two inches high it needs to be covered with four inches of dirt. Most flowers look best in groups or clumps rather than growing alone or in uh, silly little lines like they sometimes put them. This is the way nature does it, and it's a good idea to follow nature.

If you have a space in your garden two or three feet square the easy way to plant bulbs there is to simply excavate the whole area down to the proper depth and then rake the bottom with a fork and scatter bulb fertilizer in and mix it with the soil and put perhaps half an inch of soil on top and then place your bulbs in this—in this area that you've cleared. Probably place them about eight inches apart; this gives room for them to grow and to reproduce in other years. That means you won't have to dig them up for quite a number of years to, uh, pull them apart. Uh, cover them halfway up with soil and then water thoroughly, and then put the rest of the soil in and water again.

Now they need to be kept moist so if the winter, um, rains are late in coming then you need to water the spot occasionally to keep it from drying out. If you're planting individual bulbs, uh, or wanted to put bulbs in between other plants, you can dig a hole for each one with a trowel or with a bulb-planting device. Now there is a device on the market which I like very much. It's shaped kind of like a—like a tomato soup can except it's a little narrower at the bottom than at the top; sort of like a—a cone that's had the bottom of it—bottom point cut off. And at the top is fastened a handle. To plant a bulb with this you simply push it down into moist earth just like you were pushing a cookie cutter into dough, and it comes up with all the earth inside and leaves a beautiful hole just right for your bulb. You put some fertilizer in the bottom, cover it over with a little bit of soil, put the bulb in and cover it up again. That's—and then you water just as—as before.

That's really just about all you have to do. You can wait for the winter and when spring comes you'll be delighted by the growth of all these green leaves and beautiful flowers and your garden will be a total delight and you won't have to work very hard at all.

Five-Step Follow-up

Write at least one positive aspect of your interpretation.

____

Step 1 **Interpretation Rendered**

Review your entire interpretation. Select the 3-minute portion that reflects your best work. Transcribe only the portions of the interpretation you would like to improve. You do not need to transcribe the source text. Use the steps outlined below to revise each error that you identify.

____

____

____

Step 2 **Determine Underlying Reason**

Although there are many possible reasons for errors in interpretation, in this analysis you will select one of the following for each error identified in Step 1.

Comprehension

Transfer

Reformulation

Step 3 **Probable Effect of Error on Communicative Function**

After selecting the types of errors, rate each error according to how it impacts the communication, keeping in mind that not all errors are equally serious.

5 = No negative consequences to participants

4 = Consequence of errors is minimal

3 = Consequence of errors is moderate

2 = Consequence of errors is severe

1 = Consequence of errors is grave

Step 4 **Revisions**

Write, and then later record, a revised interpretation for each error that better preserves the meaning of the original source message.

Step 5 **Action Plan for Improvement**

Once you have determined the types of errors and their impact, write down what action you plan to take to improve your work.

Progress Tracking Sheet

Use this sheet to track your progress with the exercises you have completed. After performing the exercise (one or two times), answering the study questions, and doing the follow-up, fill in the tracking sheet. Note the date that you completed the exercise and give an indication of your level of accomplishment. You can use either a quantitative or a qualitative approach to track your progress.

Exercise Number	Date	First Performance	Study Questions	Follow-up Activity	Questions and Reminders	Date	Second Performance
Exercise 6.1 Quantitative							
Qualitative							
Exercise 6.2 Quantitative							
Qualitative							
Exercise 6.3 Quantitative							
Qualitative							
Quantitative Totals							

UNIT

7

Self-Monitoring and Correction

This unit focuses on monitoring your own interpretations and making corrections in your interpretation. Sometimes this process of self-correction is called repair. In simultaneous interpreting the interpreter listens to and comprehends new information in the source language while simultaneously processing previously presented information and rendering still other parts of the message into the target language. In previous units you worked to develop these simultaneous interpreting skills. In this unit you continue using and developing simultaneous interpreting skills and now check the target message for accuracy in terms of content and pronunciation and making corrections when necessary while the interpretation is ongoing. In order to know whether a correction is necessary, you must closely monitor your own interpretation for accuracy.

Moser-Mercer (1978) says that the simultaneous interpreter must process his or her own output (interpretation) in addition to processing the input (source message) and that the capacity needed to process the incoming message should not use up all of the interpreter's available capacity. When the interpreter is struggling to comprehend the message, more capacity is used at the earlier phases of the process and less capacity is left for later stages such as reformulation and monitoring. Sometimes the interpreter can catch and correct an error, but that correction may reduce the capacity to correctly process ongoing incoming information or may cause faltering.

Memory plays a role in monitoring and correction because you must remember your interpretation and compare it to the source message. Monitoring skills include listening and attending to your own output in the target language and comparing your interpretation with the source message. You must simultaneously check and remember the target language output for sense and cohesion in order to know whether corrections are necessary. A summary of some relevant aspects of memory as it relates to interpretation follows.

Memory

Memory is an important part of all phases of the interpreting process. Once you have listened intently to the source message you must remember it. It is vital that you remember the incoming message long enough to analyze and process it into the target language accurately. When you render the interpretation, you must remember your interpretation and compare that with the source message. If you decide to make a correction to the message, you must remember your repair and your original rendition in addition to the source message.

Schweda Nicholson (1996) wrote a critical review of the recent literature dealing with the role of memory in interpretation. She reviews a number of theories including those of Atkinson and Shiffrin, who proposed a model of human memory that indicates that sensory information, once perceived, is held in short-term memory (STM) for recall and is lost if not rehearsed soon after it arrives. The pace of simultaneous interpreting does not allow time to rehearse information and as a result interpreters generally do not recall what they interpret after the interpreting assignment.

Schweda Nicholson (1996) provides a summary of STM, which is also known as working memory. The duration of *working memory* is thought to be only 250 milliseconds. Baddeley and Hitch (1974) described working memory as a three-part system that is controlled by "central executive", which is served by two other systems. One is the visuospatial sketchpad, where visual and spatial images are probably created and stored. The other is the articulatory loop, which can retain limited amounts of acoustic or speech-based information. The combinations of these three aspects of working memory allow interpreters to use visualization and other strategies to assist the interpretation process.

In contrast to working or short-term memory is long-term memory (LTM). Schweda Nicholson points out that LTM has two broad categories, procedural memory and propositional memory. Procedural memory is used to perform actions such as typing or rollerblading after learning the individual actions within each skill. Once the entire set of actions has been integrated into the larger skill, it is no longer necessary to consciously focus on the performance of each action in the process. Propositional memory is the memory that allows a person to remember concepts rather than performance-based operations.

Schweda Nicholson emphasizes that there is a constant interplay between STM and LTM during the interpretation process. Interpreters can quickly access what they know about a topic and tap into memory stores related to that knowledge to help them process the incoming message.

Storing Information

Gonzalez et al. (1991) describe methods for improving retention capacity. One of the most well-known ways is by "chunking" or organizing information into units that are easier to remember. Chunking involves "dividing a message into meaningful units, possibly changing the sequence of ideas, to render it more understandable" (p. 383). This means that the interpreter does not need to remember each individual word in a sentence. Instead, the interpreter remembers the meaning of phrases or idea units. By remembering idea units instead of words, the interpreter has fewer individual units to remember and the burden on memory is reduced.

Gonzalez et al. (1991) explain that the chunking process is dependent on careful listening strategies along with the nature of the source language message and its delivery. Factors that affect listening effectiveness are density, rate, and coherence. When information is encoded in LTM, it tends to be encoded semantically or based on meaning. Information that is stored in LTM tends to be information that you perceived, found some meaning in, and had some application of that information in your life. In contrast, when information is stored in STM it tends to be encoded based on the analysis of the sounds of the words. (Baddeley, 1976, in Gonzalez et al., 1991). This fact supports the idea that when interpreters attend to the underlying message rather than just the words, memory for the message is enhanced. When you work with the exercises in this unit listen for the meaning expressed by the speakers, not just their words.

Retrieving Information

Once information is stored, the next step is retrieving the information, or finding what you need to remember. Gonzalez et al. (1991) say that the more pathways there are to items stored in memory, the more likely it is that you will be able to access the information you need to retrieve. "Memory is like a cross-referenced index card file: the more ways one has to index items or the more associations one has with items, the more pathways that lead to an item, the more likely the individual will be able to take one and find what he or she is looking for" (p. 384). Gonzalez et al. say this is why it is important for interpreters to analyze messages carefully and organize them into meaningful units by forming connections to items previously stored in memory, rather than focusing on individual words. These authors say that successful storage and retrieval of information in memory depends on whether the person wants to remember it or whether they know it will be useful to them. For example, if you really want to know how to arrive at a certain destination you will listen carefully, perhaps take notes, and possibly envision the route in your mind. If you are not responsible for the details associated with arriving at the specified location you may not attend to the details and thus not store or remember the information. You are more likely to remember information you want to remember or use frequently.

Here is a list of factors that Gonzalez et al. say affect the ways people store and retrieve information.

- If you want to remember something you are more likely to remember it.
- If the new fact is similar in some way to something you already know, you are more likely to remember it.
- If you use the information in some way you are more likely to remember it.
- You are more likely to remember the items at the beginning and end of a list or a text than the information in the middle of a text (Baddeley, 1976).
- Too much stress can reduce your ability to remember (Yerkes and Dodson, 1908).
- Moderate levels of stress can improve memory (Loftus, 1980, in Gonzalez et al., 1991).
- Irrelevant stimuli can distract you and interfere with storage and recall of information.

If an interpreter's memory skills are well developed, there is a much higher chance that the resulting interpretation will be accurate than if memory skills are weak or poorly developed. It may be that developing and practicing specific processing skills such as auditory memory, note-taking, repetition, and other skills may lead to increased effectiveness in the interpretation process. While the type of working memory processes required for interpretation could never be fully automatic, it is worthwhile to reduce the amount of effort required thorough meaningful practice.

Memory also allows the interpreter to constantly monitor the interpretation for accuracy. This means that in addition to all of the complex cognitive processes already discussed, the interpreter is continually monitoring the product and comparing it to the source language. The process of self-monitoring is very important because it allows the interpreter to realize whether an error has occurred in the interpretation. The exercises in this unit provide an opportunity to become more aware of the process of self-monitoring and correction while simultaneously interpreting.

Self-Correction

Self-correction or repair means that you provide a corrected interpretation immediately after monitoring the interpretation and determining that a correction is needed. An error in interpretation may be in the area of meaning or form. An error in understanding meaning distorts the source language message. An example of an error in form is expressing a question as a statement when it was intended as a question. Self-correction is heavily dependent on memory. You must accurately remember the source message and your interpretation in order to know whether a correction is needed.

There are several factors to check when learning to monitor and correct your own interpretations. The factors to check are intelligibility, volume, message accuracy, illocutionary force, use of fillers and repetitions, and comments on your own performance. By developing sensitivity for these factors you will be able to monitor and correct your interpretations.

Intelligibility

One factor to check for in monitoring your own work is intelligibility. This factor focuses on clear diction and pronunciation of words (or clarity of signs) and phrases in the target language. Phrases must be delivered in syntax that is appropriate to the target language. Would a user of the target language easily understand your interpretation? The target audience should not have to struggle to understand the message in the target language or further "interpret" it. Intelligibility does not include the evaluation accuracy of message transfer.

Volume

The interpretation must be loud enough for the intended audience to hear if you are working into a spoken language. If you are working into a signed language, your signs must be large enough to be easily discernible by the audience watching your interpretation.

Message Accuracy

The message conveyed in the target language must match the source language message in meaning, content, and intent. Cultural adjustments may be necessary to convey ideas appropriately in the target language. You must also take into account the composition of the target audience and their linguistic needs as well as cultural background to the extent that you can determine these factors. In order to make decisions about message equivalence you must be able to understand the message in the source language, transfer the message, and reformulate it in the target language. Language fluency in both the source and the target languages is necessary in order for you to be able to make judgments about equivalence.

Illocutionary Force

Your interpretation should convey the illocutionary force of the source message. If the source message is a question seeking information, then the interpretation should have the same effect and elicit information from the target language listener. If the source language message contains a rhetorical question, then your interpretation should reflect that although the form was a question, it does not necessarily seek information from the target audience. Likewise, statements should be rendered as statements and strong declarations in the source language should convey the same impact in the target language. The effect or impact of the message should be the same on the target audience as it was on the source language audience.

Fillers and Repetitions

Sometimes interpreters use fillers such as "um," "ah," and "hmm" or other verbalizations that are not part of the source message. Fillers are additions to the message and skew the message somewhat. Adding fillers like "um" and "ahh" show uncertainty. The target audience may assume that the speaker rather than the interpreter generates the uncertainty. Sometimes interpreters use fillers as a way to allow more time to process a message into the target language. At other times, interpreters may use fillers in response to silence on the part of the speaker. This often indicates that the interpreter is not comfortable with silence and wishes to continue verbalizing (or signing). Sometimes interpreters make repairs during a period when the speaker intends silence. This gives the impression that the speaker has made repairs to the original remarks, which skews the message and misleads the audience. It is best to preserve the illocutionary impact of silence whenever possible. Adding vocalizations like fillers can have the opposite effect of silence. If the speaker is using silence to allow time for reflection or to increase impact, then the interpreter must be confident enough to allow the silence to occur in the interpretation.

Interpreters occasionally use repetitions to attempt to repair interpretations that are not satisfactory. This can happen when the interpreter does not initially allow enough time to fully understand or process the message. When the interpreter repeats the message the target audience is likely to think that the speaker is repeating the message, when the speaker may have delivered the message only once. Then the target audience infers that the speaker is repeating the message either out of disorganization or perhaps attempting to overstate a point, when in fact neither may be true. This is an example of how the interpreter can change the impact of the message by simply repeating it. Neither the speaker nor the target audience will be aware that the interpreter, not the speaker, generated the repetition. You should avoid fillers and repetitions in interpretations.

Comments on Your Own Interpretation

Comments on your own interpretation are really another form of addition. These comments add something to the message that was not delivered by the speaker. It is common to hear interpreters or interpretation students commenting on their own interpretations, usually in unfavorable ways. But what is really going on when interpreters comment on their own work? There are very few studies that address this area. The comments interpreters make while working can reveal information about the interpreting process as well as attitudes about performance. Vik-Tuovinen (2000) studied two simultaneous interpreters' comments to each other during an interpreting assignment. The comments fell into two different categories, linguistic and extralinguistic. Linguistic comments are about the source text while extralinguistic comments are about the procedures in interpreting, or the speakers. The comments reveal how interpreters solve problems and how they prioritize problems in the interpreting booth.

While you are in training you will generally have opportunities for feedback on your interpretations. However, in daily practice as a professional, you must be able to make your own determinations about the faithfulness of your interpretations in an ongoing manner. The exercises in this unit focus on monitoring and correcting your own interpretations as you render them.

EXERCISES IN SELF-MONITORING AND CORRECTION

EXERCISE 7.1

My Early Years

THYRA BENOIT

Directions

Part of this selection appeared in an earlier volume of the *Effective Interpreting Series: English Skills Development,* where it was used as an exercise in paraphrasing. If you have worked with this text before, it is warm or familiar material. Review your work on this selection to help familiarize yourself with this passage.

This selection is approximately 3 minutes long. Find a quiet place to work where you will not be interrupted. Answer study question 1. Find the video selection. Adjust the volume as necessary and be sure you can see the TV monitor clearly. Begin by allowing yourself time to focus on the speaker's face. Record yourself simultaneously interpreting the selection. Pay close attention to your self-monitoring strategies. Do not pause or rewind the source tape. Answer the remaining study questions and complete the follow-up.

Study Questions

1. Describe the context and participants for this interpretation based on the exercise title and picture of the speaker.

___

___

2. Did the self-monitoring process distract you while you were interpreting? If so what did you do?

    ____

    ____

3. How stressful was it to consciously monitor your interpretation while interpreting this passage? Circle the answer that most closely describes your reaction and say why. Did your interpretation show your level of stress?

    Not very stressful   Stressful   Moderately stressful   Very stressful

    ____

    ____

4. Based on your impression of your interpretation, rate yourself on each of the following factors. You will examine these more closely when you complete the follow-up.

Intelligibility	Very good	Acceptable	Fair	Not acceptable
Volume	Very good	Acceptable	Fair	Not acceptable
Message accuracy	Very good	Acceptable	Fair	Not acceptable
Illocutionary force	Very good	Acceptable	Fair	Not acceptable
Fillers and repetitions	Very good	Acceptable	Fair	Not acceptable
Irrelevant comments	Very good	Acceptable	Fair	Not acceptable

5. Did correcting your interpretation cause you to lose your place in processing the incoming message? If so, what did you do?

    ____

    ____

    ____

Transcript for *My Early Years,* Thyra Benoit

Hello again. I'm Thyra Benoit: T-h-y-r-a B-e-n-o-i-t. This is part one of my story. I was born in Washington in the great year of 1950.

However, due to family difficulties my parents divorced and I moved to Watertown, Massachusetts. Some of you may know Watertown, as it is the home of the Perkins School for the Blind and the Deaf. It wasn't until I started college in 1968 that I realized that people don't cross streets with bells.

Can you imagine what it was like going to school in Boston, I attended Simmons College, and trying to cross the street with red and yellow lights flashing at the same time and hearing no bells and almost getting hit by a car? Well anyway, that was my big adventure about going to school in Boston.

At Simmons College I started as a nursing–physical therapy major, but I decided that if I wanted to graduate on time I would be better off majoring in something else, so I chose French. I liked languages and I liked to mimic people. In any case, then I had to decide what to do. I thought, well maybe I would major in French and then go on and become a social worker. But first I had to get through college, so I also took education classes.

And I had the pleasure of teaching on the high school level at an experimental school. Can you imagine what it's like to be in a classroom with the students being permitted to literally hang out of the window? Well that was acceptable.

I got through the year and then I left Boston and came to Washington, D.C., where I attended Howard University School of Social Work. I was in an experimental class, and it seems like all of my academic years have been filled with experimental first-timers. When I started school in Boston they got away—they did away with grades. And I don't know if any of you have had that experience, but it permits you to be very focused on what interests you where you can give your talents and on the mandatory subjects which don't necessarily meet your academic needs, you can get by. Well anyway, Simmons was wonderful,

I came to Howard and I learned I was in a new "thrust" class. And that meant we went straight through a two-year program, we finished in a year and a half, with no grades again. So, I'm here in Washington and I'm here to stay. And I thoroughly enjoyed my experience at Howard; it is where I met Dr. Marquessa Brown, and it is through my friendship with her that I stand before you today. Thank you.

Five-Step Follow-up

Write at least one positive aspect of your interpretation.

Step 1 Interpretation Rendered

Review your entire interpretation. Select the portion that reflects your best work. Transcribe only the portions of the interpretation you would like to improve. You do not need to transcribe the source text. Use the steps outlined below to revise each error that you identify.

Step 2 Determine Underlying Reason

Although there are many possible reasons for errors in interpretation, in this analysis you will select one of the following for each error identified in Step 1.

Comprehension

Transfer

Reformulation

Step 3 Probable Effect of Error on Communicative Function

After selecting the types of errors, rate each error according to how it impacts the communication, keeping in mind that not all errors are equally serious.

5 = No negative consequences to participants

4 = Consequence of errors is minimal

3 = Consequence of errors is moderate

2 = Consequence of errors is severe

1 = Consequence of errors is grave

____

____

Step 4 **Revisions**

Write, and then later record, a revised interpretation for each error that better preserves the meaning of the original source message.

____

____

____

Step 5 **Action Plan for Improvement**

Once you have determined the types of errors and their impact, write down what action you plan to take to improve your work.

____

____

____

EXERCISE 7.2

Making California Rolls

LESLIE RACH

Directions

This selection is approximately 3 minutes long. Find a quiet place to work where you will not be interrupted. Answer study question 1. Find the video selection. Adjust the volume as necessary and be sure you can see the TV monitor clearly. Begin by allowing yourself time to focus on the speaker's face.

Record yourself simultaneously interpreting the selection. Pay close attention to your self-monitoring strategies. Do not pause or rewind the source tape. Answer the remaining study questions and complete the follow-up.

Study Questions

1. Describe the context and participants for this interpretation based on the exercise title and picture of the speaker.

   ____

   ____

2. Did the self-monitoring process distract you while you were interpreting? If so what did you do?

   ____

   ____

   ____

3. How stressful was it to consciously monitor your interpretation while interpreting this passage? Circle the answer that most closely describes your reaction and say why. Did your interpretation show your level of stress?

   Not very stressful Stressful Moderately stressful Very stressful

   ____

   ____

4. Based on your impression of your interpretation, rate yourself on each of the following factors. You will examine these more closely when you complete the follow-up.

Intelligibility	Very good	Acceptable	Fair	Not acceptable
Volume	Very good	Acceptable	Fair	Not acceptable
Message accuracy	Very good	Acceptable	Fair	Not acceptable
Illocutionary force	Very good	Acceptable	Fair	Not acceptable
Fillers and repetitions	Very good	Acceptable	Fair	Not acceptable
Irrelevant comments	Very good	Acceptable	Fair	Not acceptable

5. Did correcting your interpretation cause you to lose your place in processing the incoming message? If so, what did you do?

____

____

____

Transcript for *Making California Rolls,* Leslie Rach

Hi, I'm Leslie Rach, and I'm going to talk today about how to make California rolls. First of all, you should assemble your ingredients, because you can get kind of caught up in all the details of this recipe. You need rice. And you don't have to have Japanese sticky rice, although it's nice, but you could use any kind of rice, except for the American converted or minute rice, or something like that. Those don't work out so well. And I usually cook my rice in a rice cooker. But we'll talk about that later. So you need rice, and you need rice vinegar. And you need nori. Those are sheets of seaweed that you'll use to roll up the rolls in. And usually, you want to use artificial crab or real crab and avocado, a ripe avocado. And for the inside part, you can put almost anything. You can use cooked carrots, or even scrambled egg.

So the first thing you do is you put your rice on, and you just follow the recipe for the cooking instructions for the rice. And at the last minute, when the rice is almost done, you put in about a cup of that rice vinegar, so it will end up being sticky and have a little more flavor than regular rice. And you get your sheets of nori, and you can roll this out on a bamboo roller, although you don't need to get so fancy. You can just do it with your bare hands on a cutting board, something like that. So, you put the rice, just a little bit in the middle of these sheets of nori in a long strip, and then you can put your fake crab sliced into, like a julienne. Same with the avocado. And you can use your cooked carrots and put those in the center. And then, you roll it up, and it sticks together itself. But, at the very end, you should take a little bit of water on your finger and just put that on the seam of the rolled up nori so that it'll stick a little better. And then, leave them rolled up. Don't cut them right away. So, you want to get all of your rolls assembled and put together and then, just before serving, you get a knife, a rather sharp knife, not with serrated edge—it works better when you have a sharp edge, but not a serrated edge—and put some water on the blade so you get a smooth cut. And then, you cut the rolls up, and you'll end up with little California rolls. And they're a big hit at parties, especially football parties and what-not, when you're mostly having people bringing chips and dip. And then you bring these California rolls. And they're a huge hit, although the kids don't like them much, especially when you serve them with wasabi, which is quite hot, but really tasty. So, next time you have a party to go to, make California rolls for your friends.

Five-Step Follow-up

Write at least one positive aspect of your interpretation.

Step 1 Interpretation Rendered

Review your entire interpretation. Select the portion that reflects your best work. Transcribe only the portions of the interpretation you would like to improve. You do not need to transcribe the source text. Use the steps outlined below to revise each error that you identify.

Step 2 Determine Underlying Reason

Although there are many possible reasons for errors in interpretation, in this analysis you will select one of the following for each error identified in Step 1.

Comprehension

Transfer

Reformulation

Step 3 **Probable Effect of Error on Communicative Function**

After selecting the types of errors, rate each error according to how it impacts the communication, keeping in mind that not all errors are equally serious.

5 = No negative consequences to participants

4 = Consequence of errors is minimal

3 = Consequence of errors is moderate

2 = Consequence of errors is severe

1 = Consequence of errors is grave

Step 4 **Revisions**

Write, and then later record, a revised interpretation for each error that better preserves the meaning of the original source message.

Step 5 **Action Plan for Improvement**

Once you have determined the types of errors and their impact, write down what action you plan to take to improve your work.

EXERCISE 7.3

Early Years of William Shakespeare

BOBBI JORDAN

Directions

This selection is approximately 9 minutes long. Find a quiet place to work where you will not be interrupted. Answer study question 1. Find the video selection. Adjust the volume as necessary and be sure you can see the TV monitor clearly. Begin by allowing yourself time to focus on the speaker's face. Record yourself simultaneously interpreting the selection. Pay close attention to your self-correction strategies. Do not pause or rewind the source tape. Answer the remaining study questions and complete the follow-up.

Study Questions

1. Describe the context and participants for this interpretation based on the exercise title and picture of the speaker.

____

____

2. Did the self-monitoring process distract you while you were interpreting? If so what did you do?

____

____

3. How stressful was it to consciously monitor your interpretation while interpreting this passage? Circle the answer that most closely describes your reaction and say why. Did your interpretation show your level of stress?

Not very stressful Stressful Moderately stressful Very stressful

____

____

____

4. Based on your impression of your interpretation, rate yourself on each of the following factors. You will examine these more closely when you complete the follow-up.

Intelligibility	Very good	Acceptable	Fair	Not acceptable
Volume	Very good	Acceptable	Fair	Not acceptable
Message accuracy	Very good	Acceptable	Fair	Not acceptable
Illocutionary force	Very good	Acceptable	Fair	Not acceptable
Fillers and repetitions	Very good	Acceptable	Fair	Not acceptable
Irrelevant comments	Very good	Acceptable	Fair	Not acceptable

5. Did correcting your interpretation cause you to lose your place in processing the incoming message? If so, what did you do?

Transcript for *Early Years of William Shakespeare,* Bobbi Jordan

Hi. My name is Bobbi Jordan. Today we're going to take a look at the early years of William Shakespeare. Now, the information that I'm going to give you is in your textbook. You have two textbooks for this course, and the first one is *Shakespeare of London* by Marchette Chute. That's spelled C-H-U-T-E. The other textbook is called *Shakespeare Alive,* and that is edited by Joseph Papp.

If we really want to understand the man, though, we have to look at the humble beginnings of his father. We've got to look at the town that he came from. You don't understand why he had such a good grasp on the common man—the porter in a play like "MacBeth" — until you know about Stratford and what it was like to live there in the years circa about 1550.

We want to take a look first, then, at John Shakespeare, William's father. John was the son of a tenant farmer. His brother was a tenant farmer. It didn't take young John very long to realize that if you farmed someone else's land you were not going to make a very good living. John had bigger ambitions. Lucky for him that he lived next to a market town called Stratford. Now, I know we're talking about 1550, but the important thing is, in terms of rural England, these were still medieval towns. They hadn't moved into, quote, the Elizabethan era. So, when we think about Stratford it's a very small town, and yet it had something really important for a man like John Shakespeare. It had a middle class.

Generally, throughout England you were either very poor or very rich. But if you could sell goods and make money at it, then you were not poor. Then you had a good living; then you belonged to a union; then you could get married and raise a good family. And that's what John Shakespeare was after.

So he moved into Stratford. He took a look around, and he said, "What do people need that I can supply?" And what they needed was gloves. Now, in modern times that would be ridiculous; we don't wear gloves very much, especially in the western states, and especially here in California. But in England: think about it. A person didn't go outside to go to work without gloves on. It would be—the parallel today would be if I were going to go to an office and I didn't wear hose, or if a man was going to go to work in a bank and he didn't have a tie on. Gloves were a commodity that everybody needed and everybody wore. So if you wanted to make money, you wanted to make something that everybody would buy.

John not only was a glover, and a very good one, he was known as a, quote, white glover. That means he made gloves out of the finest, finest lambskin and they were white as snow. So very rich people began to buy John Shakespeare's gloves. You would think that would be enough for him, but it wasn't. Because he knew he could make a good business, and he did, and he bought two houses in the middle of Stratford. And then he decided he'd better go into politics. Because he was a common man, there was no way he was going to gain glory unless he went into politics.

He first became an ale taster. Now, we think that's kind of strange, that somebody'd go around drinking beer and get paid for it, but he did. This was a time when people loved rules; you've got to understand that. There were rules for everything, and if you broke them you got fined. Let me give you some examples. If your dog was outside of your property without a muzzle you paid a fine. If your duck was caught wandering in the road you paid a fine. If you were caught playing cards you paid a fine. And suppose your children were not home by 8:00 at night, which was the curfew in Stratford—you paid a fine. You were even fined for not being in church on Sunday. And should you want to dump something on your own property—uh-uh. Everybody had to dump what they wanted to dump at the common dump at the end of the street. Why did that work so well?

Well, if you want to run a township you have to have money. And, besides, it was the kind of thing that Elizabethans, medieval people, just love. So when John became the ale taster what he did was, he went around town and checked everybody's business. It was called ale taster but he also checked the butcher's and the baker's; and actually, in the bars he made sure that the right amount of hops were used to make the beer. He made sure that when the women delivered that, that the cartons or the cases were sealed tight so nothing could get in them. And he did his job very well. He did it so well that in two more years he was made a constable.

Now he's moving up, you see. He's making good money, but he's moving up politically. During these years he also found a wife. He looked very carefully; and of course in those days it didn't matter if anybody fell in love. People got married because of land. If I have 50 acres and my neighbor has 50 acres, and I have a girl child and he has a boy child, when they're three or four years old we promise them to each other. So that when I die or when my neighbor dies, one of those kids will get not 50 acres but the two of them together will have a hundred acres. Your land was your wealth. John picked a young girl called Mary Arden. And what she brought with her were the lands of her father. So in addition to this very industrious man making money on his own, he was wise enough to marry a woman—strong, healthy, the youngest daughter—who absolutely was the apple of her father's eye, and got most of the land.

Mary and John had two children first and both of them were girls, and neither of them lived past the age of three. Now, that's not an unusual thing either, at this time in England. You—first of all, no birth control and so a woman popped babies out every year—but secondly, probably if you had 13 to 16 children only 6, maybe 5 or 6 of them made it into adulthood. And your children were as important to you as your land because the more kids you had, the more land you could acquire. So children were gems in those days, and you wanted a lot of kids. So it was a great disappointment to them that their first two daughters died. But in 1564 a son was born. And they named that son William, never ever guessing that that would be what the English world considers to be one of the greatest writers—and certainly the greatest playwright—and the man who made the English tongue respectable.

John was moving up the ladder so that by the time William was four years old his father had moved from ale taster to constable to chamberlain to high bailiff. High bailiff in Stratford is the same as the mayor. You couldn't get any higher. John had worked his way up until he was mayor of Stratford-on-Avon. Imagine being the son of the mayor. When Commedia dell'Arte troupes came through—these were touring troupes from Italy, and they were fabulous mime troupes and they had wonderful pieces of humor—who do you think had the front seat? William Shakespeare. Who do you think processed all that and collected it and put it in his brain and brought it back out again to you in "Taming of the Shrew"? William Shakespeare. I know we talk about the fact that artists suffer and live in garrets and are poor—great artists are suffering and that's why their artwork pours out, and I'm gonna tell you I think that's bunk. If you do a historical study of the great writers, musicians, painters, playwrights, of any given period from the Greeks on—gosh, their moms and dads did all right. Somebody supported them. Someone gave them a real good childhood. And a lot of them had support right on up until they made their fame.

Now that's not true with William, because William, you see, chose the theater. And his parents were very strict Protestants and once he made that choice they signed him off forever. But for the first 12 years of his life he had the world in his hands. It was a very tiny world, indeed, Stratford-on-Avon, but he had all of it as the mayor's son—going to the best Latin schools, getting the best education. Now, tomorrow we're going to follow William past the age of 12 into his teenage years—a time when he got himself into a lot of trouble, and it took a miracle to get him out.

Five-Step Follow-up

Write at least one positive aspect of your interpretation.

____

Step 1 **Interpretation Rendered**

Review your entire interpretation. Select the 3-minute portion that reflects your best work. Transcribe only the portions of the interpretation you would like to improve. You do not need to transcribe the source text. Use the steps outlined below to revise each error that you identify.

____

____

____

Step 2 **Determine Underlying Reason**

Although there are many possible reasons for errors in interpretation, in this analysis you will select one of the following for each error identified in Step 1.

Comprehension

Transfer

Reformulation

____

____

Step 3 **Probable Effect of Error on Communicative Function**

After selecting the types of errors, rate each error according to how it impacts the communication, keeping in mind that not all errors are equally serious.

5 = No negative consequences to participants

4 = Consequence of errors is minimal

3 = Consequence of errors is moderate

2 = Consequence of errors is severe

1 = Consequence of errors is grave

____

____

Step 4 **Revisions**

Write, and then later record, a revised interpretation for each error that better preserves the meaning of the original source message.

____

____

____

____

____

Step 5 **Action Plan for Improvement**

Once you have determined the types of errors and their impact, write down what action you plan to take to improve your work.

____

____

Progress Tracking Sheet

Use this sheet to track your progress with the exercises you have completed. After performing the exercise (one or two times), answering the study questions, and doing the follow-up, fill in the tracking sheet. Note the date that you completed the exercise and give an indication of your level of accomplishment. You can use either a quantitative or a qualitative approach to track your progress.

Exercise Number	Date	First Performance	Study Questions	Follow-up Activity	Questions and Reminders	Date	Second Performance
Exercise 7.1 Quantitative							
Qualitative							
Exercise 7.2 Quantitative							
Qualitative							
Exercise 7.3 Quantitative							
Qualitative							
Quantitative Totals							

References

Abbott, G., et al. (1981). *The teaching of English as an international language: A practical guide*. London: Collins.

The American Heritage Dictionary of the English Language. (1979). W. Morris (Ed.), Boston, MA: Houghton Mifflin.

Atkins, R. C., & Schriffrin, R. M. (1969). Human memory: A proposed system and its control processes. In K. W. Spence (Ed.). *The psychology of learning and motivation: Advances in research and theory*. New York: Academic Press.

Baddeley, A. D. (1976). *The psychology of memory*. New York, NY: Basic Books.

Baddeley, A., & Hitch, G. (1974). Working memory. In G. A. Bower (Ed.), *The psychology of learning and motivation*. New York, NY: Academic Press.

Bradley, J. (1981). Overconfidence in ignorant experts. Bulletin of the Psychonomic Society, 17, 82–84.

Bell, R. (1991). *Translation and translating*. New York, NY: Longman.

Berk-Seligson, S. (1987). The intersection of testimony styles in interpreted judicial proceedings: Pragmatic alterations in Spanish testimony. *Linguistics*. 25(292), 1067–1125.

Bloom, B. (1985). Generalizations about talent development. In B.S. Bloom (Ed.), *Developing talent in young people* (pp. 507–549). New York, NY: Ballantine Books.

Bonnichsen, M., & Isbell, K. (2001). The joy of boot camp for aspiring interpreters. *The Interpreter's Voice. Newsletter of the Interpreters Division of the American Translators Association*, 4, 2.

Bowen, D., & Bowen, M. (1984). *Steps to consecutive interpretation*. Washington, DC: Pen & Booth.

Chesterman, A. (2000). Teaching strategies for Emancapatory Translation. In C. Schaffner & B. Adab (Eds.), *Developing translation competence*. Benjamins (pp. 77–91). Philadelphia, PA.

Cokely, D. (1986). The effect of time lag on interpreter errors. *Sign Language Studies,* 53, 341–376.

Cokely, D. (1992). *Interpretation: A Sociolinguistic Model.* Silver Spring, MD: Linstok Press.

Conference of Interpreter Trainers (1984). New dimensions in interpeter education: Task analysis—Theory and application. In M. McIntire (Ed.), *Proceedings of the Fifth National Convention of the Conference of Interpreter Trainers. Task based approach.* Alexandria, VA: RID.

Conference of Interpreter Trainers (1996). CIT position paper: Instructional class size interpreter training. 13 (4).

Conference of Interpreter Trainers (1998). published a position pape

Cunningham, J., & Moore, D. (1986). The confused world of main idea. In J. Bauman (Ed.), *Teaching main idea identification* (pp. 1–18). Newark, DE: International Reading Association.

Danks, J., et al. (Eds.) (1997). *Cognitive processing in translation and interpreting.* Applied Psychology. Vol. 3. Thousand Oaks, CA: Sage Publications.

DeGroot, A. (2000). A complex-skill approach to translation and interpreting. In S. Tirkkonen-Condit & R. Jaaskelainen (Eds.). *Tapping and mapping the processes of translation and interpreting.* Philadelphia, PA: John Benjamins.

Dollerup, C. & Loddegaard, A. (1992). *Teaching translation and interpreting.* Philadelphia, PA: John Benjamins.

Dollerup, C. & Lindegaard, A. (1994). *Teaching translation and interpreting 2.* Philadelphia, PA: John Benjamins.

Dollerup, C., & Vibeke, A. (1996). *Teaching translation and interpreting 3.* Philadelphia, PA: John Benjamins.

Dreyfus, H. L., and Dreyfus, S. E. (1986). *Mind over machine.* Oxford: Blackwell.

Dunkel, P. G. (1985). The immediate recall of English lecture information by native and non-native speakers of English as a function of note taking. Unpublished doctoral dissertation, University of Arizona, Tucson.

Ericsson, K. (1996). The acquisition of expert performance: An introduction to some of the issues. In K. A. Ericsson (Ed.), *The road to excellence: The acquisition of expert performance in the arts and sciences, sports, and games* (pp. 1–50). Mahwah, NJ: Earlbaum.

Ericsson, K. (2001) Expertise in interpreting. *Interpreting: International Journal of Research and Practice in Interpreting,* 5 (2), 187–221.

Ericsson K., & Smith, J. (1991). Prospects and limits in the empirical study of expertise: An introduction. In K. A. Ericsson & J. Smith (Eds.), *Toward a general theory of expertise: Prospects and limits* (pp. 1–38). Cambridge, MA: Cambridge University Press.

Ericsson, K., et al. (1993). The role of deliberate practice in the acquisition of expert performance. *Psychological Review,* 100, 363–406.

Fitts, P., & Posner, M. (1967). Human performance. Belmont, CA: Brooks/ Cole.

Fabbro, F. & Gran, L. (1997). Neurolinguistic aspects of simultaneous interpretation. In Y. Gambier, D. Gile, & C. Taylor (Eds.), *Conference interpreting: Current trends in research.* Philadelphia, PA: John Benjamins.

Fleetwood, E., (1998). Personal communication.

Frauenfelder, U., & Schriefers, H. (1997). A psycholinguistic perspective on simultaneous interpreting. Interpreting: International Journal of Research and Practice in Interpreting, 2, 55–89.

Garzone, G., & Viezzi, M. (2002). *Interpreting in the 21st century: Challenges and opportunities—selected papers from the 1st Forli Conference on Interpreting Studies, 9–11 November 2000.* Philadelphia, PA: John Benjamins.

Gile. D. (1994a). Opening up in interpretation studies. In M. Snell Hornby, F. Pochhacker, & K. Kaindl (Eds.), *Translation studies—an interdiscipline. Selected papers from the Translation Studies Congress, Vienna, 9–12 September 1992,* (pp. 149–158). Philadelphia, PA: John Benjamins.

Gile, D. (1994b). The process oriented approach in the training of translators and interpreters. In C. Dollerup & A. Lindegaard (Eds.), *Teaching translation and interpreting 2.* (pp. 107–112). Philadelphia, PA: John Benjamins.

Gile, D. (1995). *Basic Concepts and Models for Intermediate and Translator Training.* Philadelphia, PA: John Benjamins.

Gile, D. (2001). The role of consecutive in interpreter training: A cognitive overview. *Communicate!* Issue 14.

Gorman (1998). Personal communication.

Gonzalez, R. et al. (1991). *Fundamentals of court interpretation: Theory, policy and practice.* Durham, NC: Carolina Academic Press.

Gopher, D., et al. (1988). Practice under changing priorities: An approach to the training of complex skills. *Acta Psychologica,* 71, 147–177.

Gopher, D. (1992). The skill of attention and control: Acquisition and execution of attention strategies. In *Synergies in experimental psychology, artificial intelligence, and cognitive neuroscience.* Cambridge, MA: MIT Press.

Hoffman, R. (1997) The cognitive psychology of expertise and the domain of interpreting. *Interpreting,* 2 (1/2), 189–230.

Howe, M. (1970). Using student's notes to examine the role of the individual learner in acquiring meaningful subject matter. *The Journal of Educational Research,* 64 (2), 61–64.

Ilg, G., & Lambert, S. (1996) Teaching consecutive interpreting. *Interpreting: International Journal of Research and Practice in Interpreting,* 1, (1) 69–99.

Ingram, R. M. (1984). Teaching decalage skills. In M. L. McIntire (Ed.), *New dialogues in interpreter education: Proceedings of the Fourth National Conference of Interpreter Trainers Convention.* (pp. 291–308). Silver Spring, MD: RID publications.

Kalina, S. (2002). Quality in interpreting and its prerequisites. In G. Garzone & M. Viezzi (Eds.), *Interpreting in the 21st century.* Philadelphia, PA: John Benjamins.

Keiser, W. (1978). Selection and training of conference interpreters. In D. Gerver & H. Sinaiko (Eds.), *Language, interpretation and communication* (pp. 251–257). Amsterdam: John Benjamins.

Kellet, C. (1995). Video-aided testing of student delivery and presentation in consecutive interpretation. *The Interpreter's Newsletter,* 6, 43–66.

Kelly, K. (1979). *The true interpreter: A history of translating theory and practice.* New York: St Martin's Press.

Klemp, G., & McClelland, D. (1986). What characterizes intelligent functioning among senior managers? In R. J. Sternberg & R. K. Wagner (Eds.), *Practical intelligence: Nature and origins of competence in the everyday world* (pp. 31–50). Cambridge, MA: Cambridge University Press.

Kohn, K., & Kalina, S. (1996). The strategic dimension of interpreting. *Meta,* 41 (1), 118–138.

Krampe, R., & Ericsson, K. (1996). Maintaining excellence: Deliberate practice and elite performance in young and older pianists. *Journal of Experimental Psychology: General,* 125, 331–359.

Kussmaul, P. (1995). *Training the translator.* Philadelphia, PA: John Benjamins.

Kurtz, I. (2002). Interpreter training programme: The benefits of coordination, cooperation, and modern technology. In E. Hung (Ed.), *Teaching translation and interpreting 4* (pp. 65–73). Philadelphia, PA: John Benjamins.

Lambert, S. (1988). A human information processing and cognitive approach to the training of simultaneous interpreters. In D. L. Hammond (Ed.), *Language at crossroads: Proceedings of the 29th Annual Conference of the American Translator's Association* (pp. 379–387). Medford, NJ: Learned Information.

Lambert, S. (1992). Aptitude testing for simultaneous interpretation at the University of Ottawa. In L. Gran & J. Dodds, (Eds.), *The interpreter's newsletter.* University of Triete: Trieste.

Larson, M. (1984). *Meaning based translation: A guide to cross-language equivalence,* Lanham, MD: University of America Press.

Loftus, E. (1980). *Memory.* Reading, MA: Addison-Welsey.

Longley, P. (1989). The use of aptitude testing in the selection of students for conference interpretation training. In L. Gran, & J. Dodds, (Eds.), *The theoretical and practical aspects of teaching conference interpretation.* Campanotto Editore: Udine.

MacWhinney, B. (1997). Simultaneous interpretation and the competition model. In J. Danks et.al. (Eds.), *Cognitive processes in translation and interpreting* (pp.215–233). Thousand Oaks, CA: Sage Publications.

Massaro, D., & Shlesinger, M. (1979). Information processing and a computational approach to SI. *Interpreting,* 2, 13–55.

Mead, P. (1994). Action and interaction in interpreting. In *The interpreter's newsletter* (pp. 19–31). Trieste, Italy: Scuola superiore di Lingue Moderne per Interpreti e Traduttori.

Merlini, R. (1994). Interpret—Consecutive interpretation module. P. 31-43. In *The interpreter's newsletter* (pp. 31–43). Trieste, Italy: Scuola superiore di Lingue Moderne per Interpreti e Traduttori.

Merriam-Webster's Encyclopedia of Literature. (1995).

Metzger, M. (2000). Sign language interpreting: Deconstructing the myth of neutrality. Washington, DC: Gallaudet University Press.

Mikkelson, H. (1983). Consecutive interpretation. *The Reflector: A Journal for Sign Language Teachers and Interpreters,* 6, 5–11.

Mikkelson, H. et al. (1991). *Fundamentals of court interpretation: Theory, policy and practice.* Durham, NC: Carolina Academic Press.

Moser-Mercer, B. (1978).Simultaneous interpretation: A hypothetical model and its practical application. In D. Gerber & H. Sinaiko (Eds.), *Language interpretation and communication* (pp. 353–368) New York: Plenum.

Moser-Mercer, B. (1996). Quality in interpreting: Some methodological issues. In *The interpreters' newsletter* (7, 43–55). Trieste, Italy: Scuola superiore di Lingue Moderne per Interpreti e Traduttori.

Moser-Mercer, B. (1997). Beyond curiosity: Can interpreting research meet the challenge? In J. Danks et al. (Eds.), *Cognitive processes in translation and interpreting* (pp. 176–196). Thousand Oaks, CA: Sage Publications.

Moser-Mercer, B., Kunzli, A., & Korac, M. (1998) Prolonged turns in interpreting: Effects on quality, physiological and psychological stress. *Interpreting,* 3 (1): 47–64.

Neubert, A. (2000). Competence in language, in languages, and in translation. In C. Schaffner & B. Adab (Eds.), *Developing translation competence* (pp. 3–19). Philadelphia, PA: John Benjamins.

Nida, E. & Taber, C. (1982). *The theory and practice of translation.* Leiden: United Bible Societies.

Niska, H. (1999). Text linguistic models for the study of simultaneous interpreting. http://www.geocities.com/~tolk/lic/LIC 990329p2.htm.

Patrie, C. (2000a). *The Effective Interpreting Series: English Skills Development.* San Diego, CA: DawnSignPress.

Patrie, C. (2000b). *The Effective Interpreting Series: Cognitive Processing in English.* San Diego, CA: DawnSignPress.

Patrie, C. (2001). *The Effective Interpreting Series: Translating from English.* San Diego, CA: DawnSignPress.

Patrie, C. (1989a). *Fingerspelled word recognition in and rapid serial visual processing in hearing adults.* Ann Arbor, MI: University Microfilms International.

Patrie, C. (1989b). Consecutive interpretation between English and American Sign Language. In D. L. Hammond (Ed.), *Coming of age: Proceedings of the 30th Annual Conference of the American Translators Association* (pp. 155–162). Medford, NJ: Learned Information.

Perfetti, C. (1985). *Reading ability.* New York: Oxford University Press.

Pochhacker, F. (1994). Quality assurance in simultaneous interpreting. In C. Dollerup & A. Lindegaard (Eds.), *Teaching translation and interpreting 2.* Philadelphia, PA: John Benjamins.

Pochhacker, F. (1995). Writings and research on simultaneous interpreting: A bibliographic analysis. *The interpreter's newsletter.* 6, 17–31.

Ramler, S. (1988). Origins and challenges of simultaneous interpretation: The Nuremberg trials experience. In D. Hammond (Ed.), *Languages at the Crossroads: Proceedings of the 29th Annual Conference of the American Translators Association* (pp. 437–440). Medford, NJ: Learned Information.

Riccardi, A. (2002a). Interpreting research: Descriptive aspects and methodological approaches. In G. Garzone & M. Viezzi (Eds.), *Interpreting in the 21st century: Challenges and opportunities: Selected papers from the first Forli Conference on Interpreting Studies, 9–11 November 2002* (pp. 15–29). Philadelphia, PA: John Benjamins.

Riccardi, A. (2002b). Evaluation in interpretation. In E. Hung (Ed.), *Teaching translation and interpreting 4.* Philadelphia, PA: John Benjamins.

Roberts, R. (1995). Student competencies in interpreting: Defining, teaching, and evaluating. In. E. A. Winston (Ed.), *Mapping our course: A collaborative venture. Proceedings of the Tenth National Convention of the Conference of Interpreter Trainers.* Charlotte, NC: Conference of Interpreter Trainers.

Rozan, J. F. (1956). *La prise de notes en interpretation consecutive.* The classical "minimalist" approach to note-taking in consecutive. Geneva: George.

Russell, D. (2002). *Interpreting in legal contexts: Consecutive and simultaneous interpreting.* Burtonsville, MD: Linstok Press.

Schweda Nicholson, N. (1985). Consecutive interpretation training: Videotapes in the classroom. *Meta,* 30 (2), 149–153.

Schweda Nicholson, N. (1988). Interpreter evaluation: The whole does not always equal the sum of its parts. In S. Wilcox (Ed.), *New dimensions in interpreter education: Evaluation and critique. Proceedings of the Seventh National Convention of the Conference of Interpreter Trainers* (pp. 65–68). Conference of Interpreter Trainers.

Schweda Nicholson, N. (1990). Consecutive note taking for community interpretation. *Interpreting—Yesterday, today, and tomorrow.* American Translators Association Scholarly Monograph, IV, 136–145. Binghamton, NY: State University of New York.

Schweda Nicholson, N. (1993) An introduction to basic note-taking skills for consecutive interpretation. In C. Nixon (Ed.), *Keystones of communication. Proceedings of the 34th Annual Conference of the American Translator's Association.* Medford, NJ: Learned Information.

Schweda Nicholson, N. (1996). Perspectives on the role of memory in interpretation: A critical review of recent literature. In M. O'Keefe (Ed.), *Global vision: Proceedings of the 37th Annual Conference of the American Translators Association.* Alexandria, VA: American Translators Association.

Schneider, W. (1985). Training high-performance skills: Fallacies and guide lines. *Human Factors,* 27, 285–300.

Seleskovitch, D. (1978a). Language and cognition. In D. Gerver & H. W. Sinaiko (Eds.), *Language interpretation and communication* (pp. 333–341). New York, NY: Plenum Press.

Seleskovitch, D. (1978b). *Interpreting for international conferences: Problems of language and communication.* Washington, DC: Pen & Booth.

Seleskovitch, D. & Lederer, M. (1989). *Pedagogie raisonee de l' interpretation.* Paris: Didier.

Seleskovitch. D., & Lederer, M. (1995). *A systematic approach to teaching interpretation.* Translated by J. Harmer. Silver Spring, MD. Registry of Interpreters for the Deaf.

Shlesinger, M. (2000). Interpreting as a cognitive process. In S. Tirkkonen-Condit & R. Jaaskelainen, (Eds.), *Tapping and mapping the processes of Translation and Interpreting: Outlooks on empirical research.* Philadelphia, PA: John Benjamins.

Seal, B. (1999). Educational interpreters document efforts to improve. *VIEWS,* 16(2), 14.

Tirkkonen-Condit, S., & Jaaskelainen, R.(2000). *Tapping and mapping the processes of translation and interpreting: Outlooks on empirical research.* Philadelphia, PA: John Benjamins.

Tommola, J. (1995). Gist recall as an aptitude test in interpreter training. In P. Krawutschke (Ed.), *Connections: Proceedings of the 36th Annual Conference of the American Translators Association* (pp. 471–382). Medford, NJ: Information Today.

Van Dam, I. (1989). Strategies of simultaneous interpretation: A methodology for the training of simultaneous interpreters. In L. Gran & J. Dodds (Eds), *The theoretical and practical aspects of teaching conference interpretation. Udine: Campnotto Editore.*

Vik-Tuovinen, G.-V. (2000). The interpreter's comments in interpreting situations. In S. Tirkkonen-Condit & R. Jaaskelainen (Eds.), *Tapping and mapping the processes of translation and interpreting: Outlooks on empirical research.* Philadelphia, PA: John Benjamins.

Widdowson, H. (1978). *Teaching language as communication.* London: Oxford University Press.

Wightman, D., & Lintern, G. (1985). Part-task training for tracking and manual control. *Human Factors,* 27, 267–283.

Witaker, R. F. (2002). Translator's/ interpreters' historic blunders along the frontiers of languages and cultures. *American Translators Association Chronicle.* Nov./Dec., 44–49.

Wortman, C. B., et al. (1988). *Psychology* (3rd Edition). New York: Alfred A. Knopf.

Yerkes, R. M., & Dodson, J. D. (1908). *The relation of strength of stimulus to rapidity of habit-formation. Journal of Comparative Neurology and Psychology,* 18, 459–482. [The origin of the Yerkes–Dodson Law.]

Zeier, H. (1997). *Psychophysical stress research. Interpreting,* 2 (1/2), 231–149.